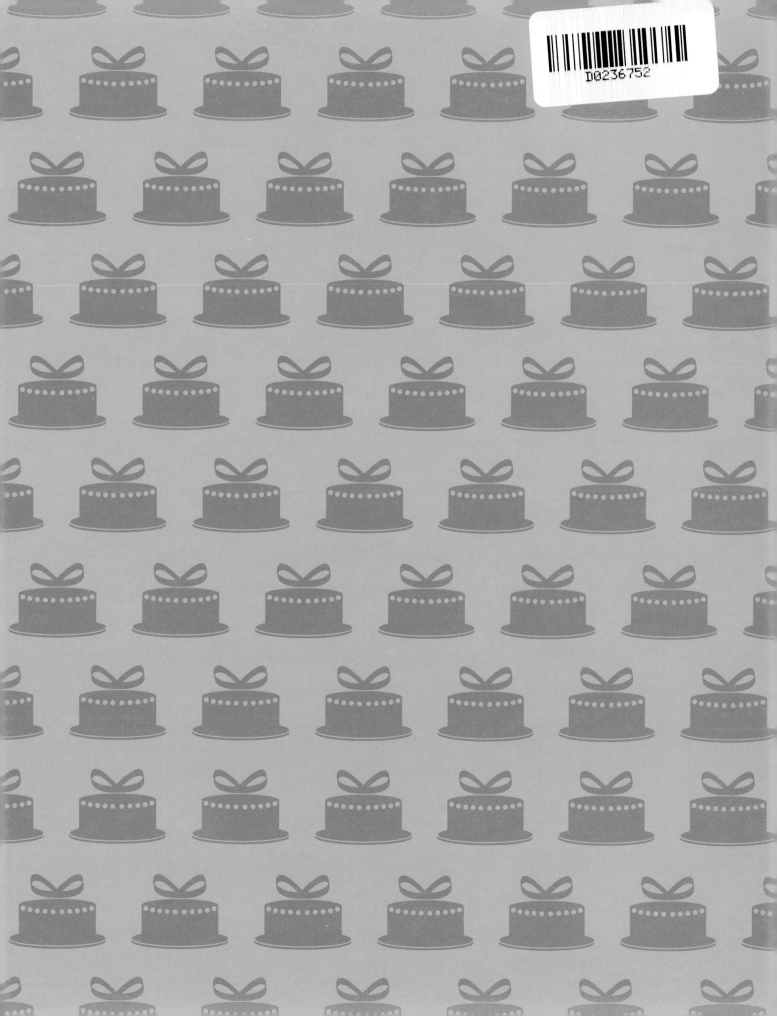

EASY CAKE DECORATING

EASY CAKE DECORATING

First edition published in 2011

LOVE FOOD is an imprint of Parragon Books Ltd

Parragon
Queen Street House
4 Queen Street
Bath BA1 1HE, UK

www.parragon.com

ISBN: 978-1-4454-2294-7

Printed in China

Author and home economist: Joanna Farrow
Photographer: Sian Irvine

Notes for the Reader
This book uses both metric and imperial measurements. Follow the same units of measurement throughout; do not mix metric and imperial. All spoon measurements are level: teaspoons are assumed to be 5 ml, and tablespoons are assumed to be 15 ml. Unless otherwise stated, milk is assumed to be full fat, eggs and individual vegetables are medium, and pepper is freshly ground black pepper.

The times given are an approximate guide only. Preparation times differ according to the techniques used by different people and the cooking times may also vary from those given. Optional ingredients, variations or serving suggestions have not been included in the calculations.

Recipes using raw or very lightly cooked eggs should be avoided by infants, the elderly, pregnant women, convalescents and anyone suffering from an illness. Pregnant and breastfeeding women are advised to avoid eating peanuts and peanut products. Sufferers from nut allergies should be aware that some of the ready-made ingredients used in the recipes in this book may contain nuts. Always check the packaging before use.

Contents

Introduction

EQUIPMENT

Most of the recipes in this book require minimal equipment, some of which you might already have. However, some specialist items are worthwhile investments, making techniques easier and improving your skills. Cake decorating shops and good kitchenware stores are useful sources, or check out the many internet suppliers.

Baking Equipment

✳ Cake Tins

Strong, sturdy, deep cake tins can be expensive but will last a lifetime. The most useful sizes for a simple birthday or Christmas cake are 20–23cm/8–9-inch round or 18–20-cm/7–8-inch square, though tiered cakes for weddings and other special occasions require two to three tin sizes. Choose tins that are at least 8-cm/3¼-inches deep so that deep cakes do not spill over the sides. Hire tins if you think you will only use them once. Other useful tins include a 12-section cupcake tray, loose-based round and square sandwich tins and a fluted Bundt tin.

✳ Paper Cupcake Cases

These are available in many different colours, patterns and sizes. The recipes in this book use cases that measure 5 cm/2 inches across the base and 4 cm/1½ inches deep. Cupcake cases do not need greasing.

✳ Electric Mixers

These make light work of mixing cake ingredients, icings and frostings. Handheld ones are easy to manage or, for large cakes, a freestanding mixer is ideal. The same results can be achieved by beating with a wooden spoon or balloon whisk but it will take longer.

✳ Mixing Bowls

An assortment of sizes is useful. Glass bowls are good for softening butter in the microwave before adding the other ingredients.

✳ Measuring Spoons

These are good for accurately measuring ingredients such as baking powder, bicarbonate of soda and cake flavourings.

✳ Kitchen Scales

Scales are essential for weighing out ingredients. Digital ones enable you to rest bowls and pans directly on the scales as you measure out the ingredients.

✳ Greaseproof and Baking Paper

These are interchangeable, though generally greaseproof paper is used for lining tins. Baking paper is stronger, ideal for making piping bags (see page 9) and for placing decorations on.

Lining a Round Cake Tin: Place the tin on greaseproof paper, draw around it and cut out.

Cut a strip of paper, at least 3 cm/1¼ inches deeper than the tin, and make a 1-cm/½-inch fold along one long edge. Snip the folded edge at 2-cm/¾-inch intervals.

Grease the tin with melted butter and fit a paper strip so the folded strip sits on the base. Cut and fit more strips to line the sides completely. Fit the circle of paper into the base. Grease the paper.

Lining a Square Cake Tin: Use the same technique as for lining a round cake tin – place the tin on greaseproof paper, draw around it and cut out. Cut a strip of paper, at least 3 cm/1¼ inches deeper than the tin, and make a 1-cm/½-inch fold along one long edge. But, this time, only snip the folded edge at the corners so the paper fits squarely into the corners of the tin.

Lining Sandwich Tins: Grease the tins and line the bases with circles or squares of greaseproof paper. Dust the greased sides of the tins with flour, tapping out the excess.

* **Pastry Brush**
A good pastry brush is useful for greasing tins and brushing cakes with glaze before decorating.

* **Kitchen Scissors**
Scissors are needed for cutting paper for lining tins, snipping tips off piping bags and cutting ribbons and other decorations.

* **Metal or Plastic Sieves**
A large sieve is useful for sifting flour and icing sugar that might have caked together in the pack during storage. A small, fine sieve or tea strainer is a more accurate way of dusting icing sugar over a cake.

* **Spatulas**
Flexible plastic spatulas are used for beating cake mixtures and icings together and for ensuring there is no wastage when scraping out mixes from bowls.

* **Wire Cooling Rack**
Most cakes are cooled on wire racks so air can circulate and cool them quickly. Cakes with a higher sugar content, such as rich fruit cake or chocolate cake, are usually cooled completely in the tin.

Decorating Equipment

Rolling Pin

A large wooden rolling pin can be used for all aspects of cake decorating, from marzipanning to rolling icings and decorations. Stainless steel, ceramic or plastic ones are less likely to damage the icing and are available in small sizes, perfect for rolling intricate decorations.

Knives and Scalpels

Use a small, sharp kitchen knife for trimming marzipan and icing. A scalpel is better for cutting out intricate icing shapes and around templates.

Palette Knife

Choose a good quality, flexible knife for spreading jam, buttercream and various icings.

Paintbrushes

A very fine-tipped brush is useful for painting fine lines and decorations. A larger brush is good for moistening surfaces and dusting.

Metal and Plastic Cutters

These are available in many different shapes and sizes, from basic round cutters to intricate flower shapes, numbers and letters.

Cake Boards

Cake boards that are 1-cm/½-inch deep are sometimes referred to as 'drums'. Available in round, square, heart and other shapes, they are strong enough to take any size cake. Thinner cake 'cards' are suitable for lightweight cakes, such as sponges, or for separating tiers when stacking a cake.

Cocktail Sticks

These are useful for dotting tiny amounts of food colouring into icing and easing soft icing or melted chocolate into corners.

Icing Smoother

This is a flat plastic tool that creates a perfectly smooth surface when applying ready-to-roll icing. These are available in two different styles – a general purpose one for both the top and sides of a cake and one specifically for smoothing the sides of a cake.

✳ Turntable
Resting a cake, on its board or plate, on a turntable enables you to turn the cake very easily as you decorate.

✳ Ruler
Use a metal or plastic ruler for making piping bags, measuring tin and cutter sizes and accurately gauging spaces between decorations.

✳ Plastic Dowels
Dowels are used to support the tiers of a stacked wedding or celebration cake.

✳ Tweezers
A small pair of tweezers is useful for securing small decorations, such as silver balls.

✳ Wallpaper Scraper
These can be used for making chocolate caraque (see page 42). Keep one specifically for this purpose.

✳ Piping Bags
These are easy to make from baking or greaseproof paper and can also be bought in paper, clear film or re-usable nylon. To make a paper piping bag, cut out a 25-cm/ 10-inch square from baking paper and fold the paper diagonally in half to make a triangle. Cut the paper in half, just to one side of the folded line to make two triangles. Hold one triangle with the long edge away from you and curl the right point over to meet the central point, forming a cone shape. Curl the left point over the cone so the three points meet. Adjust the points if necessary so there's no hole at the tip of the cone. Fold the points over to secure the cone in place.

✳ Piping Nozzles
Nozzles are available in a wide range of sizes and designs. Large nozzles are used for piping generous swirls of buttercream or frosting onto cupcakes. Smaller nozzles are used for piping stars, lines, dots or writing. The recipes in this book use a large star nozzle, 1 cm/½ inch across the tip, a smaller 5-mm/¼-inch star nozzle and a fine writer nozzle.

BASIC CAKE RECIPES

Rich Chocolate Cake

This cake is rich, moist and easy to slice. Once cool, wrap in foil and store in a cool place for up to three days or freeze. Unwrap and leave overnight to defrost before decorating.

Round tin	10-cm/4-inch	15-cm/6-inch	20-cm/8-inch	25-cm/10-inch
Square tin	8-cm/3¼-inch	13-cm/5-inch	18-cm/7-inch	23-cm/9-inch
Cocoa powder	25 g/1 oz	55 g/2 oz	100 g/3½ oz	175 g/6 oz
Boiling water	100 ml/3½ fl oz	200 ml/7 fl oz	300 ml/10 fl oz	550 ml/19 fl oz
Plain chocolate, chopped	70 g/2½ oz	125 g/4½ oz	250 g/9 oz	400 g/14 oz
Lightly salted butter, softened	55 g/2 oz	100 g/3½ oz	200 g/7 oz	350 g/12 oz
Light muscovado sugar	125 g/4½ oz	250 g/9 oz	500 g/1 lb 2oz	750 g/1 lb 10 oz
Eggs, beaten	1	2	4	6
Plain flour	100 g/3½ oz	175 g/6 oz	375 g/13 oz	550 g/1 lb 4 oz
Bicarbonate of soda	½ tsp	½ tsp	¾ tsp	1½ tsp
Vanilla extract	1 tsp	2 tsp	4 tsp	2 tbsp
Baking time at 160°C/325°F/ Gas Mark 3	1 hour	1½ hours	2 hours	2¾ hours
Serves	4	10	20	30

1. Preheat the oven to 160°C/325°F/ Gas Mark 3. Grease and line the required cake tin (see page 7). Put the cocoa in a heatproof bowl and gradually whisk in the boiling water until smooth. Immediately tip in the chocolate and leave to cool, stirring the mixture frequently until the chocolate melts.

2. Put the butter and sugar in a large mixing bowl and whisk with an electric mixer to soften. Add the eggs, flour, bicarbonate of soda and vanilla and beat until combined. Stir in the chocolate mixture until evenly mixed. Spoon into the prepared tin and smooth the surface.

3. Bake in the preheated oven for the time stated above, or until firm to the touch and a skewer inserted into the centre comes out nearly clean. Leave to cool in the tin.

Vanilla Sandwich Cake

This is a moist, buttery sponge. It can be stored in an airtight container for 1–2 days before decorating, but should be frozen if keeping for longer. Defrost overnight before decorating. These cakes can be sandwiched with buttercream (and jam if desired), cream cheese frosting or chocolate ganache before decorating.

Round sandwich tins	2 x 10-cm/4-inch	2 x 15-cm/6-inch	2 x 20-cm/8-inch	2 x 25-cm/10-inch
Square sandwich tins	*	*	2 x 18-cm/7-inch	2 x 23-cm/9-inch
Lightly salted butter, softened	60 g/2¼ oz	115 g/4 oz	280 g/10 oz	500 g/1 lb 2 oz
Caster sugar	60 g/2¼ oz	115 g/4 oz	280 g/10 oz	500 g/1 lb 2 oz
Eggs, beaten	1	2	5	9
Vanilla extract	½ tsp	1 tsp	1 tbsp	2 tbsp
Self-raising flour	60 g/2¼ oz	115 g/4 oz	280 g/10 oz	500 g/1 lb 2 oz
Milk	2 tsp	1½ tbsp	3 tbsp	5 tbsp
Baking time at 180°C/350°F/Gas Mark 4	15 minutes	25 minutes	35–40 minutes	45–50 minutes
Serves	4	8	16	26

*Square sandwich tins are not available in these sizes. To make sponge cakes in these sizes, use deep cake tins and bake half the mixture at a time.

1. Preheat the oven to 180°C/350°F/Gas Mark 4. Grease and line the required tins (see page 7). Put the butter and sugar in a mixing bowl and beat with an electric mixer until creamy and very pale.

2. Gradually beat in the eggs, adding a little at a time so the mixture doesn't start to separate. If it does, beat in a little of the flour. Stir in the vanilla extract.

3. Sift the flour into the bowl and stir in gently with a large metal spoon. Stir in the milk. Divide between the prepared sandwich tins and smooth the surfaces. Bake in the preheated oven for the time stated above, or until the surface feels just firm to the touch.

4. Loosen the edges of the cakes with a knife and turn out onto a wire rack to cool.

Flavour Variations

For each egg in the quantity chart above, add the following ingredients (beating in after the eggs):

Lemon - finely grated zest of ½ lemon, plus lemon juice to replace the milk.

Orange - finely grated zest of ¼ orange, plus orange juice to replace the milk.

Almond - add ¼ tsp almond extract and substitute 15 g/½ oz flour with 15 g/½ oz ground almonds.

Vanilla Cupcakes

MAKES 12

✦ Preparation time:
10 minutes
✦ Cooking time:
20–25 minutes

INGREDIENTS

✻ 150 g/5½ oz lightly
salted butter, softened
✻ 150 g/5½ oz caster
sugar
✻ 3 eggs
✻ 150 g/5½ oz
self-raising flour
✻ 2 tsp vanilla extract
✻ 1 tbsp milk

Cupcakes are the easiest to make of all cakes.
There is no greasing or lining of tins and the
sponge is mixed together in one easy stage.
Paper and silicone cupcake cases come in
an interesting range of colours and designs
so choose ones that suit your decorations or
party colour scheme. For sizes, see page 6.

1. Preheat the oven to 180°C/350°F/Gas
Mark 4. Line a 12-section bun tray with paper
cupcake cases. Put all of the ingredients in a
mixing bowl and beat with an electric mixer
for 1–2 minutes until the mixture is smooth
and creamy.

2. Divide the
mixture among
the cases, making
sure you fill each
case fairly evenly
and only three-
quarters fill each
case. Bake in the
preheated oven for
20–25 minutes, or
until the surface
feels just firm to the
touch. Transfer to wire racks to cool.

For chocolate cupcakes: substitute 25 g/1 oz of
the flour for 25 g/1 oz of cocoa powder.

Carrot Cake

SERVES 12–14

✦ Preparation time:
25 minutes
✦ Cooking time:
30–40 minutes

INGREDIENTS

✻ 175 g/6 oz carrots
✻ 100 g/3½ oz fresh
pineapple, chopped
✻ 175 g/6 oz lightly salted
butter, softened
✻ 200 g/7 oz light
muscovado sugar
✻ 3 eggs, beaten
✻ 225 g/8 oz self-raising
flour
✻ 2 tsp baking powder
✻ ½ tsp bicarbonate
of soda
✻ 1½ tsp ground
cinnamon
✻ 100 g/3½ oz ground
almonds
✻ 55 g/2 oz sultanas

This is a deliciously moist cake, perfect for any
occasion from teatime to a special birthday.
It will keep fresh in an airtight container for
a couple of days but it is best to freeze it, if
stored for longer. Once decorated, it will keep
fresh in a cool place for up to 5 days.

1. Preheat the oven to 180°C/350°F/Gas Mark
4. Grease and line 2 x 20-cm/8-inch sandwich
tins (see page 7), each at least 4 cm/1½ inches
deep. Finely grate the carrots. Finely chop the
pineapple.

2. Put the butter and sugar in a mixing bowl
and beat with an electric mixer until smooth
and creamy. Gradually beat in the eggs, adding
a little at a time so the mixture doesn't start to
separate. If it does, beat in a little of the flour.

3. Sift the flour, baking powder, bicarbonate
of soda and cinnamon into the bowl and stir
in gently with a large metal spoon. Add the
almonds, sultanas, carrots and pineapple and
stir in until evenly combined. Divide equally
between the tins and smooth the surface.

4. Bake in the preheated oven for about 30–40
minutes, or until risen and just firm to the touch.
A skewer inserted into the centres of the cakes
should come out clean. Leave in the tins for 10
minutes then transfer to a wire rack to cool.

Rich Fruit Cake

Once cooked and cooled, fruit cake should be wrapped in greaseproof paper and a double thickness of foil. Store the cake in a cool, dry place for 1–3 months. Before storing, if desired, unwrap and pierce the cake all over with a skewer and drizzle with 2–4 tablespoons of additional liqueur (depending on the size of the cake). Rewrap and repeat during the storage period, as desired. Rich fruit cake is also delicious served freshly baked, although it is less easy to slice.

Round tin	10-cm/4-inch	15-cm/6-inch	20-cm/8-inch	25-cm/10-inch
Square tin	8-cm/3¼-inch	13-cm/5-inch	18-cm/7-inch	23-cm/9-inch
Mixed dried fruit	250 g/9 oz	600 g/1 lb 5 oz	1 kg/2 lb 4 oz	1.8 kg/4 lb
Brandy, sherry or orange juice	2 tbsp	4 tbsp	100 ml/3½ fl oz	150 ml/5 fl oz
Lightly salted butter, softened	55 g/2 oz	125 g/4½ oz	250 g/9 oz	425 g/15 oz
Dark muscovado sugar	55 g/2 oz	125 g/4½ oz	250 g/9 oz	425 g/15 oz
Eggs, beaten	1	2	5	9
Plain flour	85 g/3 oz	200 g/7 oz	350 g/12 oz	550 g/1 lb 4 oz
Ground mixed spice	1 tsp	2 tsp	5 tsp	2 tbsp
Black treacle	2 tsp	1 tbsp	2 tbsp	4 tbsp
Natural glacé cherries, halved	30 g/1 oz	55 g/2 oz	100 g/3½ oz	175 g/6 oz
Blanched almonds, chopped	30 g/1 oz	55 g/2 oz	100 g/3½ oz	175 g/6 oz
Baking time at 140°C/275°F/ Gas Mark 1	1¼–1½ hours	2¼–2½ hours	3¼–3½ hours	4–4¼ hours
Serves	6	16	30	50

1. Grease and line the required cake tin (see page 7). Put the mixed dried fruit in a mixing bowl and stir in the liqueur or juice. Cover and leave to stand for several hours or overnight until the liquid has been absorbed, stirring once or twice.

2. Preheat the oven to 140°C/275°F/Gas Mark 1. Put the butter and sugar in a mixing bowl and whisk with an electric mixer until pale and creamy. Gradually add the beaten eggs, whisking well between each addition. Add a little of the flour if the mixture starts to separate.

3. Sift the flour and spice into the bowl and stir in until combined. Stir in the black treacle then the steeped fruit and any unabsorbed liqueur, plus the cherries and almonds.

4. Spoon into the prepared tin and smooth the surface. Tie a double thickness of brown paper around the outside of the tin (this prevents the edges overcooking before the centre is cooked through). Bake in the preheated oven for the time stated above, or until a skewer inserted into the centre comes out clean. Leave to cool completely in the tin.

ICINGS AND FROSTINGS

The icings and frostings on these two pages are those most frequently used in this book. See individual recipes for how to use and store.

Buttercream

MAKES 1 QUANTITY (250 g/9 oz)

◆ Preparation time: 5 minutes

INGREDIENTS
✳ 100 g/3$\frac{1}{2}$ oz unsalted butter, softened
✳ 150 g/5$\frac{1}{2}$ oz icing sugar
✳ 1 tbsp hot water

This simple buttercream can be spread with a palette knife or is easy to pipe, both in fine lines or generous swirls. Store in the refrigerator in a sealed container for up to a week and allow to come to room temperature before use.

1. Put the butter in a mixing bowl and beat with an electric mixer to soften. Add the icing sugar and beat well until smooth and creamy.

2. Add the hot water and beat again until very soft and fluffy in texture.

Flavour Variations
Lemon – use 2 tbsp lemon juice instead of the water and add the finely grated rind of 1 lemon.
Orange – use 2 tbsp orange juice instead of the water. Add finely grated rind of 1 small orange.
Chocolate – blend 25 g/1 oz cocoa powder with 2 tbsp boiling water to make a paste. Add to the buttercream with 2 tsp vanilla extract and beat until smooth and creamy.

Covering Cakes with Buttercream
Cakes can be spread with buttercream as a decoration or prior to covering with ready-to-roll icing. If using as a decoration, spread thinly with a palette knife first and chill for 15 minutes to seal in the crumbs. Then spread with a thicker, even layer of buttercream. Add texture by tilting the palette knife at an angle to create ridges or spread smoothly by holding the palette knife flat.

Cream Cheese Frosting

MAKES 1 QUANTITY (250 g/9 oz)

◆ Preparation time: 10 minutes

INGREDIENTS
✳ 100 g/3$\frac{1}{2}$ oz full-fat cream cheese
✳ 50 g/1$\frac{3}{4}$ oz unsalted butter, softened
✳ 1 tsp lemon juice
✳ 100 g/3$\frac{1}{2}$ oz icing sugar

This is traditionally used as a filling and covering for carrot cake but is also delicious with chocolate cake or vanilla sponge. It is easy to spread and pipe and keeps for a few days in the refrigerator before use. Cakes decorated with this frosting are best eaten within two days.

1. Beat together the cream cheese and butter with an electric mixer until smooth.

2. Add the lemon juice and icing sugar and beat again until the frosting is light and creamy.

Royal Icing

Royal icing can be bought in packs but homemade royal icing is easy to mix and keeps well for several days in the fridge. Place in an airtight container and seal with clingfilm so it doesn't dry out. Royal icing is good for spreading and piping and gradually sets hard. To stop this hardening, beat in 1 teaspoon of glycerine for each egg white used.

1. Put the egg white in a bowl with a little icing sugar. Beat well until smooth.

2. Gradually beat in the remaining icing sugar to give a soft, peaking consistency. Transfer to a container and cover tightly with clingfilm. To colour royal icing, use a cocktail stick to dot a little food colouring onto the icing and whisk in.

MAKES 1 QUANTITY (250 g/9 oz)

✦ Preparation time: 10 minutes

INGREDIENTS
✳ 1 egg white
✳ 200 g/7 oz icing sugar, sifted

Ready-to-Roll Icing

This is available in a wide range of colours from supermarkets or the internet. Home-made ready-to-roll icing stores for up to a week in a cool place, but must be thoroughly wrapped in clingfilm to prevent a crust forming. Lightly knead before use.

1. Put the egg white, glucose and 100 g/3½ oz of the icing sugar in a large bowl and mix with an electric mixer or a wooden spoon until smooth.

2. Gradually work in more icing sugar until the paste becomes too stiff to mix. Turn out onto a surface dusted with icing sugar and gradually knead in more icing sugar with your hands until you have a smooth, very firm paste. If it's too soft, the icing will be sticky and difficult to roll out. Wrap thoroughly in clingfilm until ready to use.

To colour homemade or bought ready-to-roll icing, dust the work surface with icing sugar and knead the paste lightly to soften. Dot the icing with food colouring using a cocktail stick. Knead until evenly coloured, working in more colour for a darker shade.

MAKES 700 g/1 lb 9 oz

✦ Preparation time: 15 minutes

INGREDIENTS
✳ 1 egg white
✳ 2 tbsp liquid glucose
✳ approx 625 g/1 lb 6 oz icing sugar

USING CHOCOLATE

Chocolate is one of the most exciting cake ingredients to work with, not only for its delicious flavour and glossy texture but also its versatility as a frosting and decoration. Chocolate ganache, a chocolate cream frosting, makes a delicious cake covering while melted chocolate can be shaped, moulded or piped into sculptural creations, both simple and intricate.

❋ Melting Chocolate
Chocolate can be melted in the microwave or on the hob. Both methods work well, although you are better able to control the heating temperature of chocolate melted on the hob, particularly milk and white chocolate which scorch easily if overheated.

To melt on the hob, chop the chocolate into small pieces and put in a heatproof bowl. Rest the bowl over a saucepan of gently simmering water, making sure that the base of the bowl does not sit in the water. Once the chocolate starts to melt, turn off the heat and leave until the chocolate is melted and smooth, stirring occasionally. Lift the bowl away from the pan, ensuring that no drips of water get into the bowl as this will make the chocolate 'seize', making it dull and solidified. To melt in the microwave, chop the chocolate, put in a microwave proof bowl and heat on medium power, in 1 minute sessions, stirring gently after each heating so the chocolate melts evenly.

Dark Chocolate Ganache

MAKES 1 QUANTITY
(500 g/1 lb 2 oz)

◆ Preparation time:
5 minutes, plus cooling

INGREDIENTS
❋ 250 g/9 oz plain chocolate, chopped
❋ 250 ml/9 fl oz double cream
❋ 2 tbsp icing sugar

This luxurious frosting is a smooth blend of chocolate and cream. It is easiest to use once cooled and thickened but not starting to set. If it does firm up before you're ready to use it, place the bowl over a pan of hot water, stirring frequently until softened.

1. Put the chocolate in a bowl. Heat the cream and sugar in a saucepan until beginning to bubble around the edges (but not boiling) and pour over the chocolate.

2. Leave to stand, stirring frequently until the chocolate has melted and the ganache is smooth and glossy. It can be used as soon as it's cool enough to hold its shape.

For white chocolate ganache: use the same quantites as dark, but heat only half the cream to pour over the white chocolate. Once the chocolate has melted and the mixture is completely cold, stir in the remaining cream. Whisk lightly with an electric mixer until the ganache just holds its shape. Do not over-mix or the texture will be spoiled.

✳ To Make Chocolate Curls

Use a potato peeler and pare off thick curls of chocolate from a bar. The curls can be made thicker by using a chunky bar of chocolate and by angling the peeler to get thicker curls.

If the chocolate is so cold that it breaks off in brittle pieces, warm very briefly for a few seconds in the microwave.

Chocolate caraque is another type of chocolate curl, usually reserved for special occasion cakes. See page 42 for how to make caraque.

✳ To Make a Chocolate Collar

A chocolate collar looks impressive encasing a special occasion cake. Before making the collar, have the cake ready on its serving plate or board and freshly spread with ganache, cream or buttercream.

Measure around the circumference of the cake with a piece of string. Cut a piece of acetate that is 1 cm/ ½ inch longer than the string and 1 cm/½ inch deeper than the cake. Spread the acetate with melted plain, milk or white chocolate, leaving 1 cm/½ inch uncovered at one short end. Spread the chocolate right to the edges of one long edge. The chocolate along the other edge can be spread in a wavy line or with a paintbrush to give an uneven edge.

Leave the collar on the surface until the chocolate has thickened but is not beginning to set. It should take about 15 minutes but keep lifting the edge of the collar to check how runny the chocolate is.

Lift the collar around the cake so the long straight edge sits on the base. For larger cakes you might need to ask someone to help you with positioning the collar. Secure the acetate at the ends with tape so the uncovered end overlaps the other. Leave to set completely in a cool place until the acetate can be peeled away.

CAKE DECORATING TECHNIQUES

The following techniques are easy to master with practice and feature repeatedly throughout this book. After covering with marzipan or icing, the iced cakes should ideally be left overnight to set before decorating.

✱ Covering the Top with Marzipan

Apricot glaze is spread over cakes before marzipanning to hold the marzipan in place. To make, press the required amount of apricot jam (see chosen recipe) through a sieve into a small pan and add 1 teaspoon of water or brandy for every 2 tablespoons of jam. Heat gently until smooth.

Brush the top of the cake with the apricot glaze. Lightly knead the marzipan on a surface dusted with icing sugar to soften. Reserve half of the marzipan, wrapped in clingfilm, and roll out the remainder until 5 cm/2 inches larger than the diameter of the cake. Transfer to a sheet of baking paper. Invert the cake onto the marzipan and press the paste up against the sides of the cake to fill the gaps around the edges. Use a sharp knife to cut off the excess marzipan to leave a neat edge, reserving the trimmings. Turn the cake the right way up and place on a plate, cake card or board (see chosen recipe).

✱ Covering the Sides with Marzipan

Measure around the cake's circumference with a piece of string. Brush the sides of the cake with apricot glaze. Knead the trimmings with the reserved marzipan and roll out to a strip slightly longer than the string and slightly wider than the depth of the cake. Cut to the exact length and depth of the cake and roll up the paste. Place against the side of the cake and unroll, pressing it into position and butting the ends together.

✱ Covering with Ready-to-Roll Icing

Roll out icing on a surface lightly dusted with icing sugar until at least 13 cm/5 inches larger than the diameter of the cake. Keep lifting and turning as you work so it doesn't stick. Using the rolling pin, lift the icing over the cake so it falls evenly down the sides. Use your hands to ease the icing around the cake so there are no creases and the icing fits snugly around the base of the cake. Trim off any excess with a knife, held vertically against the side of the cake. Dust an icing smoother with icing sugar and use a circular motion to smooth the icing flat on top then around the sides. Keep working the smoother until the icing is completely flat, trimming off any excess that builds up around the base. If any air bubbles appear, pop with a pin and re-smooth. Leave to set overnight.

✴ Covering a Cake Board

Covering the exposed top edge of the cake board with icing gives a professional looking finish. Thinly roll out the required amount of ready-to-roll icing on a surface lightly dusted with icing sugar to a long, thin, curved strip. Trim off the inner edge of the strip with a knife. Dampen the edges of the board with water and lift the strip into position so the cut edge rests against the side of the cake. Overlap the two ends and cut through with a knife. Lift away the trimmings and smooth out the join with your fingers. Smooth the icing around the edge of the board and trim off the excess with a knife.

✴ Basic Piping Techniques

Buttercream and ganache are easy to pipe whether from a large or small piping nozzle. The consistency of royal icing can be altered according to the type of shapes to be piped. When piping stars, make sure that royal icing holds its shape when stirred with a spoon. Piping fine lines or tiny dots is easier to do if the icing is thinned with a few drops of water to give a softer consistency.

✴ Stacking Cakes

If you are making a three-tier stacked cake, it is best to 'dowel' the cakes to give support and prevent a potential collapse! Place a small bowl, plate or cake card centrally on the large cake and mark around it with the tip of a knife or scalpel. Push a plastic dowel down into the cake, just inside the marked circle, making sure it goes right through to the cake base. Make a pencil mark to show the height of the cake. Lift out the dowel and saw through the pencil mark with a hacksaw or bread knife. Cut three more dowels to exactly the same height and push the dowels into the cake, evenly spacing them inside the marked circle. Repeat the process with the middle tier. Spread a little royal icing into the marked circles before stacking the cakes.

CUPCAKES & SMALL CAKES

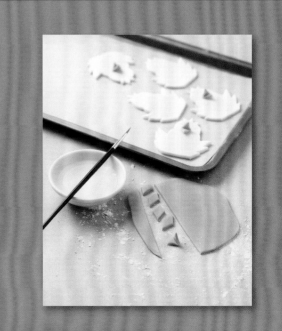

Flower Cupcakes

MAKES 12

◆ Preparation time:
10 minutes, plus cooling
◆ Cooking time:
20–25 minutes
◆ Decoration time:
45 minutes

INGREDIENTS

✹ 1 quantity buttercream, see page 14
✹ black food colouring
✹ yellow food colouring
✹ 12 vanilla cupcakes, see page 12, baked in pink cases
✹ 50 g/1¾ oz black ready-to-roll icing, see page 15
✹ icing sugar, for dusting
✹ 50 g/1¾ oz pink ready-to-roll icing, see page 15

The combination of pink, black and yellow on these cupcakes is both modern and pretty, though you can choose any other colour scheme to suit a particular occasion.

1. Place 2 tablespoons of the buttercream in a small bowl and beat in a little black food colouring. Put the remainder of the buttercream in a second bowl and beat in a little yellow food colouring. Set aside 2 tablespoons of the yellow buttercream. Using a palette knife, spread the bowl of yellow buttercream over the cupcakes, doming it up slightly in the centres.

2. Line a baking sheet with baking paper. Roll out the black icing thinly on a surface very lightly dusted with icing sugar. Press a 1-cm/½-inch flower plunger cutter into the icing. Lift away the cutter and transfer the icing shapes to the prepared baking sheet, pressing out the shape with the plunger. Shape about 55 more black flowers in the same way.

3. Roll out the pink icing thinly on a surface lightly dusted with icing sugar. Create about 55 pink flowers, using the method in Step 2. Arrange all of the flowers over the buttercream, placing about nine on each cupcake.

4. Put the black buttercream and reserved yellow buttercream in two paper piping bags (see page 9). Snip off just the very ends of the tips so that the icing can be piped in tiny dots. Pipe a dot of black into the pink flowers and yellow into the black flowers.

TOP TIP
The flowers can be shaped well in advance. Once hardened, store them in an airtight container between layers of kitchen paper for up to two weeks.

Animal Print Cupcakes

MAKES 12

◆ Preparation time:
10 minutes, plus cooling

◆ Cooking time:
20–25 minutes

◆ Decoration time:
1 hour

INGREDIENTS

✳ 12 chocolate cupcakes,
see page 12, baked in
black or brown cases

✳ 1 quantity chocolate
buttercream, see page 14

✳ 85 g/3 oz black
ready-to-roll icing,
see page 15

✳ icing sugar, for dusting

✳ 85 g/3 oz white
ready-to roll icing,
see page 15

✳ 85 g/3 oz brown
ready-to-roll icing,
see page 15

✳ 85 g/3 oz yellow
ready-to-roll icing,
see page 15

Bring a little animal magic to teatime with these fun cupcakes. Cute animal prints are rolled into contrasting colours of icing to make professional looking patterns.

1. Using a palette knife, spread the cupcakes with the buttercream in a fairly smooth layer.

2. Set aside a small piece of the black icing then roll out the remainder thinly on a surface lightly dusted with icing sugar. Place the icing on a chopping board. Using a small sharp knife, cut out small, wavy-edged shapes in varying sizes, ranging from about 1–2.5 cm/½–1 inch across. Make about 15 shapes and set aside any remaining trimmings. Set aside a small piece of white icing and thinly roll out the remainder as above. Lay the black shapes over the white icing, leaving a little space between each. Dust the rolling pin and roll it over the icing so the black icing is pressed into the white. Cut out circles with a 7.5-cm/3-inch round cutter from this black and white icing and lay them over four of the cupcakes.

3. Set aside a small piece of the brown icing and thinly roll out the remainder, as above. Take the reserved black icing, a small piece of yellow icing and the reserved white icing and roll each under your fingers into long thin ropes

(these can be of uneven thickness). Lay the ropes over the brown icing in irregular lines. Roll, cut out circles using a 7.5-cm/3-inch round cutter and lay them over four more cupcakes.

4. Thinly roll out the remaining yellow icing, as before. Roll half of the reserved brown icing into balls the size of small peas. Space them about 4 cm/1½ inches apart over the yellow icing. Roll smaller balls of the remaining brown icing (as small as you can) and position four of these tiny balls, about 5 mm/¼ inch apart, around one side of each of the pea-sized balls. Roll, cut out circles and position over the four remaining cupcakes, as before.

TOP TIP
Use a very light dusting of icing sugar, particularly when rolling out black icing, so it doesn't 'cloud' the icing.

Easter Chick Cupcakes

MAKES 12

♦ Preparation time:
10 minutes, plus cooling
♦ Cooking time:
20–25 minutes
♦ Decoration time:
1 hour, plus overnight
setting

INGREDIENTS
❋ 250 g/9 oz yellow
ready-to-roll icing,
see page 15
❋ icing sugar, for dusting
❋ 30 g/1 oz orange
ready-to-roll icing,
see page 15
❋ 200 g/7 oz white
chocolate
❋ blue food colouring
❋ 12 chocolate cupcakes,
see page 12, baked in
brown cases
❋ 1 quantity chocolate
buttercream, see page 14

These chirpy chicks provide a splash of colour and fun – and are great as either a springtime or Easter gift.

1. Trace and cut out the Easter chick template (see pages 94–95). Line a baking sheet with baking paper. Roll out half of the yellow icing thinly on a surface lightly dusted with icing sugar and transfer to a chopping board. Lay the template over the icing and carefully cut around it with a scalpel or sharp knife. Cut five more chicks in the same way, transferring the shapes to the prepared baking sheet. Re-roll the trimmings and the remaining yellow icing and create 7–8 more chicks in the same way as above (the extras are in case of any breakages).

2. Roll out the orange icing thinly on a surface lightly dusted with icing sugar and cut out 14 small diamond shapes, using a sharp knife or scalpel. Bend these diamonds almost in half and position on the chicks' heads, securing with a dampened paintbrush. Leave the chicks overnight to harden.

3. Use the white chocolate to make white chocolate curls (see page 17).

4. Dilute a little blue food colouring with a drop of water and use to paint eyes on the chicks. Using a palette knife, spread the cupcakes with the buttercream. While the buttercream is still soft, peel the paper away from the chicks and press the chicks gently down onto the cupcakes so they are held in place by the buttercream. Scatter the chocolate curls around the chicks.

TOP TIP
If you are not confident with painting the eyes with a brush, try using a blue icing pen, available from cake decorating shops.

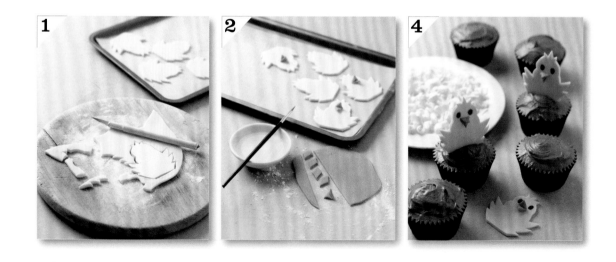

New Baby Cupcakes

MAKES 12

◆ Preparation time:
10 minutes, plus cooling
◆ Cooking time:
20–25 minutes
◆ Decoration time:
1 hour

INGREDIENTS

✳ 150 g/5½ oz white
ready-to-roll icing,
see page 15
✳ icing sugar, for dusting
✳ 150 g/5½ oz pale blue
or pink ready-to-roll icing,
see page 15
✳ 1 tbsp apricot jam
✳ 12 vanilla cupcakes,
see page 12, baked in blue
or pink cases
✳ tube of white
writing icing

These pretty cupcakes can be made with either pink or blue icing to suit the gender of the new baby – or any other colour that you prefer!

1. Thinly roll out the white icing on a surface lightly dusted with icing sugar. Using a 7.5-cm/3-inch cutter, stamp out six rounds. Repeat with the blue or pink icing. Make apricot glaze with the jam (see page 18). Brush each cupcake lightly with a little of the glaze and gently press an icing round on top.

2. Re-roll the blue or pink icing trimmings. Use a small teddy bear cutter to stamp out two teddy bears. Use a tiny flower cutter to stamp out four flowers.

3. Re-roll the white icing trimmings. Use a small flower cutter to stamp out two small flowers. Use a 4-cm/1½-inch fluted cutter to stamp out two rounds, then cut away a small oval from each round to resemble a baby's bib. Use a 2.5-cm/1-inch cutter to stamp out two rounds and mark with the end of a paintbrush to resemble buttons. Shape four booties and two ducks from the remaining icing trimmings.

4. Attach all the decorations to the top of the cupcakes using a dampened paintbrush. Use the writing icing to add the finishing touches, such as bows on the booties.

TOP TIP
The decorations can be adapted to suit whichever cutters you already have in your kitchen drawer.

Cupcake Wedding Cake

MAKES 36

✦ Preparation time:
30 minutes, plus cooling
✦ Cooking time:
1–1¼ hours
✦ Decoration time:
1½ hours

INGREDIENTS
✴ 36 vanilla cupcakes,
see page 12, baked in
white cases
✴ 2 quantities
buttercream, see page 14
✴ 800 g/1 lb 12 oz white
ready-to-roll icing,
see page 15
✴ icing sugar, for dusting
✴ 100 g/3½ oz green
ready-to-roll icing,
see page 15

Anyone can tackle decorating a wedding cake when it's made entirely of cupcakes! Multiply the quantity of cakes so it's right for the number of guests and change the bow decoration colours to tie in with the colour scheme of the wedding.

1. Using a palette knife, cover the cupcakes with buttercream in a fairly smooth layer. Roll out 250 g/9 oz of the white icing thinly on a surface lightly dusted with icing sugar. Cut out circles using a 7.5-cm/3-inch round cutter and press gently onto the cupcakes. Gather up the trimmings and re-roll with a further 250 g/9 oz of the icing until all of the cupcakes are covered.

2. To make the bows, roll out a 70-g/2½-oz piece of white icing, as above, to a 15-cm/6-inch square. Thinly roll out 25 g/1 oz of the green icing until 15 cm/6 inches long. Cut into 5-mm/¼-inch strips and lay the strips over the white icing, leaving a tiny gap between each.

3. Roll the rolling pin over the icing to flatten the green icing into the white.

4. Use a sharp knife to cut vertically down the middle of the green parts of the icing to create thin green-edged lengths of icing. For each bow, cut 2 x 2.5-cm/1-inch lengths from the icing and position on a cupcake for bow ends, securing in place with a dampened paintbrush. Cut 2 x 5-cm/2-inch lengths, bend into loops, pinching the ends together, and position above the bow ends. Secure as above. Cut a further 1-cm/½-inch square of icing, shape into a cube and position in the middle of the bow to form the knot. Secure as above. Repeat with the remaining cut icing lengths, then roll and shape more bows using the remaining white and green icing until all the cupcakes are decorated.

TOP TIP
These cakes look stunning arranged on a tiered cupcake or cake stand. Arrange a posy of small white flowers in the centre of the tiers.

Snowflake Cupcakes

MAKES 12

- ◆ Preparation time: 10 minutes, plus cooling
- ◆ Cooking time: 20–25 minutes
- ◆ Decoration time: 1½ hours, plus 24 hours setting

INGREDIENTS

- ✳ 2 quantities royal icing, see page 15
- ✳ edible white glitter flakes
- ✳ finely grated rind and juice of 2 limes
- ✳ 3 tbsp caster sugar
- ✳ 12 vanilla cupcakes, see page 12, baked in blue cases
- ✳ 3 tbsp lime or lemon preserve
- ✳ 225 g/8 oz marzipan
- ✳ icing sugar, for dusting

These delicate snowflake cakes, dusted with sparkling glitter, will take pride of place on the kitchen table. Don't be put off by the intricate style of the piping – once you've done one, the rest will definitely get easier!

1. Line a large baking sheet or board with baking paper. Trace the snowflake template (see pages 94–95) and slide the traced template under the baking paper. Take a quarter of the royal icing and check that it is the right consistency for piping (see page 19). Spoon this icing into a piping bag fitted with a writer nozzle (see page 9). Pipe over all the lines of the snowflake template and scatter with edible glitter flakes while still soft. Move the template around and pipe 12–13 more snowflake shapes onto the baking paper. Leave to harden for 24 hours.

2. Heat the lime rind and juice in a small saucepan with the caster sugar until dissolved. Using a skewer, pierce holes all over the cupcakes and drizzle with the syrup. Press the preserve through a sieve into the pan and add 1 tablespoon of water. Heat gently until the preserve has melted. Brush the mixture over the cupcakes.

3. Thinly roll out the marzipan on a surface lightly dusted with icing sugar. Cut out circles using a 7.5-cm/3-inch round cutter and lay them over the cupcakes, re-rolling the trimmings to make more rounds.

4. Using a palette knife, spread the remaining royal icing over the cupcakes. Carefully peel the baking paper away from the snowflakes and place the snowflakes gently on each cupcake.

TOP TIP
You'll need 12 snowflakes in total but it's worth piping two or three extra in case of breakages. Always peel the paper away from delicate icing shapes, rather than the shape away from the paper, to avoid breaking them.

Lemon & Almond Fondants

MAKES 16

◆ Preparation time:
15 minutes, plus cooling
◆ Cooking time:
25–30 minutes
◆ Decoration time:
1½ hours, plus setting

INGREDIENTS
✳ 175 g/6 oz lightly
salted butter, softened,
plus extra for greasing
✳ 175 g/6 oz caster sugar
✳ 3 eggs
✳ 150 g/5½ oz self-
raising flour
✳ 1 tsp almond extract
✳ 30 g/1 oz ground
almonds

TO DECORATE
✳ 4 tbsp caster sugar
✳ 3 tbsp lemon juice
✳ 1 quantity lemon
buttercream, see page 14
✳ 500 g/1 lb 2 oz fondant
icing sugar
✳ yellow and pink
food colouring
✳ 8 pale yellow and
8 pale pink sugar roses,
see page 76

These little cakes are just perfect for a special tea. They also make a great present, arranged in a shallow box.

1. Preheat the oven to 180°C/350°F/Gas Mark 4. Grease and line 2 x 18-cm/7-inch square sandwich cake tins (see page 7). Put the butter, caster sugar, eggs, flour, almond extract and ground almonds in a bowl and beat with electric beaters until smooth and creamy. Divide the mixture between the prepared tins and bake in the preheated oven for 25–30 minutes, or until just firm to the touch. Transfer to a wire rack to cool.

2. To decorate, mix together the caster sugar and lemon juice. Leave to stand for 10 minutes, or until the sugar dissolves. Sandwich the cakes together with half of the buttercream and spoon over the lemon syrup. Using a large sharp knife, trim off a 5-mm/¼-inch slice from the edges of the cake then cut the cake into 16 squares.

3. Using a palette knife, spread the remaining buttercream on top of each square, doming the buttercream up in the centre.

4. Beat the fondant icing sugar with 5–6 tablespoons of cold water to make a smooth paste that thickly coats the back of a metal spoon. Divide between two bowls and colour half the paste pale yellow and half pale pink.

5. Place the squares on a wire rack. Using a teaspoon, drizzle the yellow icing over eight cakes so it runs down the sides, coating most of the sponge (don't worry if there are areas of sponge still visible). Cover the remaining cakes with pink icing. Leave the squares to set, then decorate with the sugar roses.

TOP TIP
If made a day in advance, the cake will be much easier to cut and decorate.

Chocolate Ice-Cream Cones

MAKES 8

✦ Preparation time:
45 minutes
✦ Cooking time:
20–25 minutes
✦ Decoration time:
30 minutes

INGREDIENTS
✹ 1 egg white
✹ 55 g/2 oz light muscovado sugar
✹ 1 tbsp plain flour
✹ 2 tbsp cocoa powder
✹ 2 tbsp double cream
✹ 30 g/1 oz lightly salted butter, melted
✹ 1 quantity dark chocolate ganache, see page 16
✹ 100 g/3½ oz shop-bought chocolate sponge cake
✹ sugar sprinkles, to decorate

Crisp chocolate wafer cones, filled with chocolate sponge and creamy chocolate ganache make an indulgent fix for any serious chocolate lover!

1. Preheat the oven to 200°C/400°F/Gas Mark 6. To make the cones, line a baking sheet with baking paper. Put the egg white and sugar in a bowl and whisk until combined. Add the flour, cocoa, cream and butter and mix to a smooth paste.

2. Place 2 tablespoons of the mixture, spaced well apart, on the prepared sheet. Spread each mixture with the back of a spoon into a round, about 12 cm/4½ inches in diameter.

3. Bake in the preheated oven for 5–6 minutes until the surface looks dry and has a slightly bubbly surface. Leave to cool for 1 minute. Peel away one round from the paper and roll into a cone shape. As the cone cools, it will start to firm up but you might find it easier to push a cone of kitchen paper into the chocolate cone and leave it supporting the shape until it cools. Repeat with a second batch, then bake and shape in the same way, using new baking paper each time. Repeat to create eight cones in total.

4. Put the ganache into a large piping bag fitted with a 1-cm/½-inch star nozzle (see page 9). Pipe a little into each cone until about one-third full. Spread this up the sides with a knife so the insides of the cones are covered in a thin layer of ganache. Crumble the chocolate sponge into the cones.

5. Pipe large swirls of the remaining chocolate ganache into the tops of the cones and finish with sugar sprinkles.

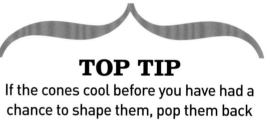

TOP TIP
If the cones cool before you have had a chance to shape them, pop them back very briefly in the oven to soften so they are easier to roll up.

CAKES FOR ALL OCCASIONS

2

Frosted Fruits Cake

SERVES 16

◆ Preparation time:
25 minutes, plus cooling
◆ Cooking time:
35–40 minutes
◆ Decoration time:
40 minutes, plus chilling

INGREDIENTS

✷ 2 x 20-cm/8-inch round vanilla sandwich cakes, see page 11
✷ 5 tbsp raspberry or strawberry jam
✷ 150 ml/5 fl oz double cream
✷ pink food colouring
✷ 2 quantities cream cheese frosting, see page 14
✷ 350–400g/12–14 oz summer fruits, such as strawberries, raspberries and blueberries
✷ icing sugar, for sprinkling

This impressive cake is perfect for a summer afternoon tea or as a dessert after a leisurely lunch. Use firm, undamaged fruits so their juices don't seep into the frosting.

1. Place one of the cakes on a flat serving plate and spread with the jam. Using an electric mixer, whip the cream until it is just holding its shape. Spread the cream over the jam, almost to the edges of the cake. Position the second cake on top and press down gently so the cream is level with the edges of the cake.

2. Beat a dash of pink food colouring into the cream cheese frosting to colour it the palest shade of pink. Using a palette knife, spread a very thin layer over the top and sides of the cake to seal in the crumbs. The cake will still show through at this stage but will be covered by the second layer of frosting. Chill in the refrigerator for 15 minutes.

3. Use the palette knife to spread a thicker layer of frosting around the sides of the cake. Spread the remainder over the top. Once evenly covered, use the edge of the palette knife to swirl the frosting as smoothly or as textured as you like.

4. Arrange the fruits on top of the cake. Put a little icing sugar in a small, fine sieve and gently tap it over the fruits to lightly frost.

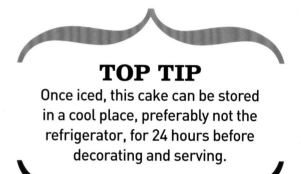

TOP TIP
Once iced, this cake can be stored in a cool place, preferably not the refrigerator, for 24 hours before decorating and serving.

Chocolate Caraque Cake

SERVES 20

✦ Preparation time:
25 minutes, plus cooling

✦ Cooking time:
2 hours

✦ Decoration time:
35 minutes, plus chilling

INGREDIENTS

✹ 200 g/7 oz plain chocolate, chopped

✹ 20-cm/8-inch round rich chocolate cake, see page 10

✹ 6 tbsp brandy (optional)

✹ 2 quantities dark chocolate ganache, see page 16

✹ rose petals or small edible flowers, to decorate (optional)

Making chocolate caraque is a baking skill that's easy to achieve and adds a professional looking touch to cakes and desserts. Caraque keeps in an airtight container for two weeks without spoiling, layered between sheets of greaseproof paper.

1. Melt the chocolate (see page 16) and spread it in a thin layer on a marble slab or clean, smooth surface such as a plastic chopping board. Leave in a cool place until the chocolate is set but not brittle.

2. Push a clean wallpaper scraper or the edge of a palette knife across the surface of the chocolate, holding it at about 30° so that the chocolate starts to roll into loose curls. If the chocolate is too cold, it will break off in brittle shards and should be left at room temperature for a while before you try again. Transfer the caraque to a baking sheet lined with baking paper and chill in the refrigerator while you finish the cake.

3. Slice the cake in half horizontally. Drizzle the tops of the cake halves with brandy, if using.

4. Use quarter of the chocolate ganache to sandwich the cake layers together and place the cake on a flat serving plate or cake stand. Spread a thin layer of ganache around the sides of the cake with a palette knife to seal in the crumbs. Chill in the refrigerator for 15 minutes. Spread the remaining ganache all over the cake in an even layer, smoothing it so it is as flat or as textured as you like.

5. Scatter the chocolate caraque over the cake so the pieces fall at different angles. Scatter with rose petals or small edible flowers, if using.

TOP TIP
A small marble slab is a worthwhile investment if you do a lot of chocolate work as its cool surface helps chocolate to set.

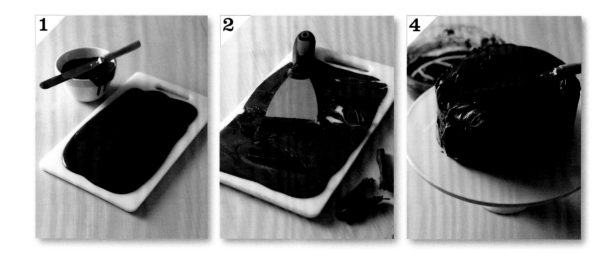

Chocolate Ganache Cake

SERVES 10

◆ Preparation time:
25 minutes, plus cooling
◆ Cooking time:
40 minutes
◆ Decoration time:
1 hour, plus chilling

INGREDIENTS

✳ 175 g/6 oz butter, plus extra for greasing
✳ 175 g/6 oz caster sugar
✳ 4 eggs, lightly beaten
✳ 250 g/9 oz self-raising flour
✳ 1 tbsp cocoa powder
✳ 50 g/1¾ oz plain chocolate, melted
✳ 2 quantities dark chocolate ganache, see page 16
✳ 200 g/7 oz plain chocolate, chopped

This simple and light chocolate cake looks visually impressive with the piped ganache topping and a chocolate collar around the outside.

1. Preheat the oven to 180°C/350°F/Gas Mark 4. Grease and line the base of a 20-cm/8-inch round springform cake tin (see page 7).

2. Beat the butter and sugar until light and fluffy. Gradually add the eggs, beating well after each addition. Sift the flour and cocoa powder together. Fold into the cake mixture. Fold in the melted chocolate. Spoon into the prepared tin and smooth the top. Bake in the preheated oven for 40 minutes, or until springy to the touch. Leave the cake to cool for 5 minutes, then turn out onto a wire rack. Cut into two layers.

3. Reserve one third of the dark chocolate ganache. Use the remaining ganache to sandwich the cake together and spread over the top and sides of the cake.

4. Melt the chopped chocolate (see page 16) and use to create a chocolate collar around the cake (see page 17). Leave to cool until just set. Create a paper piping bag (see page 9) and pipe the reserved ganache onto the cake in tear-shaped drops.

TOP TIP
Wait for 2 hours, or until the ganache is firm, light and fluffy, before piping the shapes over the cake.

Coffee Bundt Cake

SERVES 12–14

◆ Preparation time:
30 minutes, plus cooling
◆ Cooking time:
50 minutes
◆ Decoration time:
20 minutes

INGREDIENTS
❋ 400 g/14 oz plain flour,
plus extra for dusting
❋ 1 tbsp baking powder
❋ 1 tsp bicarbonate
of soda
❋ 3 tbsp espresso
coffee powder
❋ 275 g/9¾ oz lightly
salted butter, softened,
plus extra for greasing
❋ 125 g/4½ oz light
muscovado sugar
❋ 225 ml/8 fl oz maple
syrup
❋ 3 eggs, beaten
❋ 225 ml/8 fl oz
buttermilk
❋ 225 ml/8 fl oz double
cream

TO DECORATE
❋ 4 tbsp maple syrup
❋ 200 g/7 oz icing sugar
❋ 15 g/½ oz unsalted
butter, melted
❋ 20 chocolate-coated
coffee beans

Bundt cakes cook quickly and, therefore, stay deliciously moist due to the hole through the centre of the tin. The flavour combination of coffee and maple syrup is just delicious!

1. Preheat the oven to 180°C/350°F/Gas Mark 4. Grease a 3-litre/5¼-pint Bundt tin. Dust the base and sides with flour, tipping out the excess.

2. Sift the flour, baking powder, bicarbonate of soda and coffee powder into a bowl. In a separate bowl, beat together the butter and muscovado sugar with an electric mixer until pale and creamy. Gradually whisk in the maple syrup. Beat in the eggs slowly, adding 3 tablespoons of the flour mixture to prevent curdling.

3. Mix together the buttermilk and cream and add half to the butter mixture. Sprinkle in half of the flour mixture and fold gently together. Add the remaining buttermilk and flour mixtures and mix together gently until just combined.

4. Spoon into the prepared tin and smooth the surface. Bake in the preheated oven for about 50 minutes, or until well risen and a skewer inserted into the centre comes out clean. Leave in the tin for 10 minutes, then loosen with a knife and invert onto a wire rack to cool completely.

5. To make the icing, beat the maple syrup in a bowl with 150 g/5½ oz of the icing sugar and the butter, until smooth and thickly coating the back of a wooden spoon. Transfer the cake to a serving plate and spoon the icing around the top of the cake so it starts to run down the sides.

6. Beat the remaining icing sugar in a small bowl with 1½–2 teaspoons of water to make a smooth paste. Using a teaspoon, drizzle the icing over the cake. Scatter the coffee beans over the top.

TOP TIP
If you don't have a classic Bundt tin, use any other ring tin with the same capacity.

Flower Power

◆ Preparation time:
25 minutes, plus cooling

◆ Cooking time:
40 minutes

◆ Decoration time:
1 hour, plus overnight setting

INGREDIENTS

✺ 2 x carrot sandwich cakes, see page 12

✺ 1 quantity buttercream, see page 14

✺ 700 g/1 lb 9 oz lime green ready-to-roll icing, see page 15

✺ 150 g/5½ oz white ready-to-roll icing, if covering cake board, see page 15

✺ 70 g/2½ oz each of white, pink, orange and yellow ready-to-roll icing, see page 15

✺ icing sugar, for dusting

✺ small bowl of pink, yellow and orange candy-coated chocolate sweets

✺ 1 m/3⅓ feet pink or yellow ribbon, 1 cm/½ inch wide (optional)

This funky, fun cake will appeal to every girl from one to 91! Once decorated, it will keep in a cool place for several days.

1. Sandwich the two carrot cakes together with half of the buttercream. Place on a 28-cm/11-inch round cake board (or use a flat plate that complements the colours of the decoration). Spoon 3 tablespoons of the buttercream into a small paper piping bag fitted with a writer nozzle (see page 9). Using a palette knife, spread the remaining buttercream over the top and sides of the cake.

2. Use the lime green icing to cover the cake (see page 18) and the white icing to cover the cake board, if using (see page 19). Leave to firm up overnight before decorating, if desired.

3. Roll out the white, pink, orange and yellow icing thinly on a surface lightly dusted with icing sugar. Cut out flower shapes with a selection of cutters (see Top Tip).

4. Secure the flowers to the cake by moistening the backs of the flowers with a dampened paintbrush and pressing gently onto the icing. Build up the design into a trail that curls into a point on the top of the cake and thickens out around the sides. The design will start to look effective as you add more flowers to the cake, mixing up the colours and shapes.

5. Secure the sweets in the centre of some of the flowers with dots of buttercream from the piping bag. Add further dots of buttercream to the centres of the remaining flowers. Wrap the ribbon around the cake board, if using, securing with a dressmaker's pin.

TOP TIP
Use 4–5 different-sized flower cutters and, for the best effect, use a mixture of fluted and pointed cutters.

Shopper's Heaven

SERVES 16

◆ Preparation time:
25 minutes, plus cooling

◆ Cooking time:
35–40 minutes

◆ Decoration time:
1¼ hours, plus overnight
setting

INGREDIENTS

✴ 2 x 18-cm/7-inch
square lemon sandwich
cakes, see page 11

✴ 1 quantity lemon
buttercream, see page 14

✴ 6 tbsp lemon curd

✴ 800 g/1 lb 12 oz white
ready-to-roll icing,
see page 15

✴ 150 g/5½ oz black
ready-to-roll icing,
see page 15

✴ 85 g/3 oz each of deep
pink, pale grey and green
ready-to-roll icing,
see page 15

✴ icing sugar, for dusting

✴ ½ quantity royal icing,
see page 15

✴ black food colouring

✴ 1 m/3⅓ feet pink or
grey ribbon, 1 cm/½ inch
wide

Do you have a friend who thrives on retail therapy? This could be the perfect cake choice to entice her away from the shops! Dresses, shoes and handbags look effective, though you can easily create your own designs.

1. Sandwich the cakes together with half of the buttercream and all of the lemon curd. Place the cake on a 28-cm/11-inch square cake board. Using a palette knife, spread the remaining buttercream over the top and sides of the cake.

2. Use the white icing to cover the cake (see page 18) and the black icing to cover the cake board (see page 19). Leave to firm up overnight before decorating, if desired.

3. Trace and cut out the dress, shoe and handbag templates (see pages 94–95). Roll out half the pink, grey and green icings thinly on a surface lightly dusted with icing sugar and transfer to a chopping board. Lay the templates over the icing and cut around each with a scalpel or sharp knife. Repeat with the remaining icings.

4. Once you've cut several shapes, moisten the backs with a dampened paintbrush and press them gently onto the cake, leaving a small gap between them. Cover the rest of the cake in the same way, trimming off the shapes with a scalpel where they extend over the base of the cake.

5. Colour the royal icing black (see page 15) and put in a piping bag fitted with a writer nozzle (see page 9). Pipe buttons on the dresses and details on the handbags. Wrap the ribbon around the cake board, securing with a dressmaker's pin.

TOP TIP
A lightweight plastic chopping board is ideal for cutting out icing shapes with a scalpel. If this slips on the work surface, rest it over a tea towel.

Chocolate Drizzle Cake

SERVES 20

◆ Preparation time:
40 minutes, plus cooling

◆ Cooking time:
1½ hours

◆ Decoration time:
45 minutes, plus setting

INGREDIENTS

✳ 2 x 15-cm/6-inch round
rich chocolate cakes,
see page 10

✳ 2 quantities white
chocolate ganache,
see page 16

✳ 1 tbsp unsalted butter

✳ 1 tbsp golden syrup

✳ 100 g/3½ oz plain
chocolate, chopped

✳ 400 g–500 g/14 oz–1 lb
2 oz plain, milk and white
chocolate truffles

Our love affair with chocolate is exemplified in this party centrepiece – an intensely decadent creation, from the richly flavoured sponge to its lavish decoration.

1. Slice each cake in half horizontally and sandwich all the layers together with a quarter of the chocolate ganache. Place all the layers on a flat serving plate.

2. Spread a thin layer of ganache around the sides of the cake with a palette knife to seal in the crumbs. Chill in the refrigerator for 15 minutes. Spread the remaining ganache all over the sides in an even layer. Leave to firm up in a cool place for at least an hour.

3. Put the butter and syrup in a small pan and heat gently until the butter has melted. Add the chocolate and heat very gently until the chocolate starts to melt. Remove from the heat and stir until the chocolate has melted completely. Spoon into a small bowl and leave until cool and slightly thickened, but not starting to set.

4. Tip the chocolate out over the top of the cake and ease it to the edges with a palette knife. Use the back of a teaspoon to gently nudge the chocolate over the edges of the cake so it starts to run down the sides. Repeat all round the top of the cake.

5. Leave in a cool place for at least an hour to firm up before piling the chocolate truffles on top.

TOP TIP

This cake looks most effective if the chocolate is drizzled down the sides unevenly. Do this by nudging varying amounts of the chocolate mixture over the top edges of the cake.

Chocolate Tiered Cake

SERVES 34

◆ Preparation time:
1 hour, plus cooling
◆ Cooking time:
3¼ hours
◆ Decoration time:
1¼ hours, plus overnight
setting

INGREDIENTS
✴ 2 quantities dark
chocolate ganache,
see page 16
✴ 8 chocolate cupcakes,
see page 12, baked in
blue cases
✴ 25-cm/10-inch and
10-cm/4-inch round
rich chocolate cakes,
see page 10
✴ 1.3 kg/3 lb shop-bought
chocolate ready-to-roll
icing
✴ icing sugar, for dusting
✴ 100 g/3½ oz each of
blue and green ready-
to-roll icing, see page 15
✴ handful of blue, green
and brown candy-coated
chocolate sweets
✴ 50 cm/20 inch blue
ribbon, 1 cm/½ inch wide

This colourful, fun cake offers guests the choice between either a ganache-laden cupcake or a chunky slice of chocolate cake.

1. Put a third of the chocolate ganache in a large piping bag fitted with a 1-cm/½-inch star nozzle (see page 9) and pipe swirls onto the cupcakes. Place the large chocolate cake on a 33-cm/13-inch cake board. Put the small chocolate cake on a baking sheet lined with baking paper.

2. Spread the remaining ganache over the top and sides of both cakes, using a palette knife to spread it in a smooth layer.

3. Roll out 900 g/2 lb of the chocolate ready-to-roll icing thinly on a surface lightly dusted with icing sugar and use to cover the large cake (see page 18). Reserve the trimmings. Cover the small cake with a further 300 g/10½ oz of the icing. Once you have trimmed off the excess icing from around the base, carefully position the small cake on top of the large one, in the centre. Use the trimmings and the remaining icing to cover the cake board (see page 19). Leave to firm up overnight before decorating, if desired.

4. Thinly roll out half the blue and green icings, as before, and cut out a selection of circles using small round cutters. Position them around the sides of the cakes, securing in place with a dampened paintbrush. Roll out any trimmings and the remaining icings to make more circles.

5. Arrange seven of the cupcakes around the edge of the lower tier and one on the top tier, scattering them with the sweets. Wrap the blue ribbon around the base of the larger cake and the cake board, securing with a dressmaker's pin.

TOP TIP
The blue and green decorations look great against the chocolate icing but you can adapt the colour scheme to suit.

Pretty In Pink

SERVES 24

◆ Preparation time:
45 minutes, plus cooling
◆ Cooking time:
1 hour
◆ Decoration time:
2 hours, plus overnight
setting

INGREDIENTS
✳ 2 x 20-cm/8-inch and
2 x 15-cm/6-inch round
vanilla sandwich cakes,
see page 11
✳ 8 tbsp raspberry or
strawberry jam
✳ 2 quantities
buttercream, see page 14
✳ 700 g/1 lb 9 oz pale
pink ready-to-roll icing,
see page 15
✳ icing sugar, for dusting
✳ 800 g/1 lb 12 oz deep
pink ready-to-roll icing,
see page 15
✳ ½ quantity royal icing,
see page 15
✳ 1.5 m/5 feet pale cream
ribbon, 1 cm/½ inch wide
✳ bag of pearl balls
✳ 1 m/3⅓ feet fluffy
pink trim

This cute cake will impress any young girl for a variety of occasions. Simple cut out hearts and pearl balls are easy to secure, making it well within the grasp of first time decorators.

1. Sandwich the large cakes together with 5 tablespoons of the jam and 7 tablespoons of the buttercream and place on a 25-cm/10-inch round cake board. Sandwich the small cakes together with the remaining jam and a further 5 tablespoons of the buttercream. Place on a 15-cm/6-inch cake card.

2. Using a palette knife, spread the tops and sides of both cakes with the remaining buttercream. Use the pale pink icing to cover the large cake (see page 18). Dust a surface lightly with icing sugar and roll out 550 g/1 lb 4 oz of the deep pink icing. Use this deep pink icing to cover the small cake (see page 18). Put a teaspoon of the royal icing on the centre of the large cake and spread it slightly. Position the small cake on top. Use 150 g/5½ oz of the deep pink icing to cover the cake board (see page 19). Leave to firm up overnight before decorating, if desired.

3. Put the remaining royal icing in a paper piping bag (see page 9) and snip off just the tip. Wrap the cream ribbon around the base of the small cake so it overlaps slightly. Trim and set aside the remaining ribbon. Secure the ribbon around the small cake with a dot of royal icing.

4. Thinly roll out half the remaining deep pink icing and cut out small heart shapes using 1-cm/½-inch and 2-cm/¾-inch heart-shaped cutters. Moisten the backs of the hearts with a dampened paintbrush and secure over the large cake. Gather up the trimmings and roll out with the remaining deep pink icing and cut out a further 2–3 heart shapes using a slightly larger cutter. Place on a sheet of baking paper to harden for at least 2 hours.

5. Pipe small dots of royal icing, about 1 cm/½ inch apart, onto the small cake and press a pearl ball gently onto each. Wrap more cream ribbon around the cake board, securing with a dressmaker's pin.

6. Secure the pink trim around the large cake with a dot of royal icing. Coil more pink trim on top of the cake, securing with royal icing and tucking in the large pink hearts to finish.

Giant Cupcake

SERVES 10

✦ Preparation time:
20 minutes, plus cooling

✦ Cooking time:
1¼ hours

✦ Decoration time:
1¼ hours, plus overnight setting

INGREDIENTS

✹ butter, for greasing

✹ 15-cm/6-inch round rich chocolate cake mixture, see page 10, uncooked

✹ 1 quantity chocolate buttercream, see page 14

✹ 500 g/1 lb 2 oz blue ready-to-roll icing, see page 15

✹ icing sugar, for dusting

✹ 15 g/½ oz each of pink, blue, white and yellow ready-to-roll icing, see page 15

✹ 150 g/5½ oz fondant icing sugar

✹ 30 g/1 oz red ready-to-roll icing, see page 15

✹ confectioners' glaze, see Top Tip

This must be the only cupcake in the world to serve 10 hungry cake lovers!

1. Preheat the oven to 160°C/325°F/Gas Mark 3. Grease and line a 1-litre/1¾-pint ovenproof pudding basin with greaseproof paper. Spoon the cake mixture into the basin and bake in the preheated oven for 1¼ hours, or until a skewer inserted into the centre comes out clean. Leave to cool in the basin.

2. Slice the domed surface off the top of the cake and crumble into a bowl. Beat 3 tablespoons of the buttercream into the bowl, cover and set aside in a cool place. Invert the remaining cake onto a chopping board lined with baking paper and spread with the remaining buttercream. Roll out the blue icing on a surface dusted with icing sugar to a 30-cm/12-inch round. Lift the icing over the cake and ease it to fit neatly around the sides. Trim off the excess around the base. While the icing is still soft, take an unridged pencil and press it into the icing all around the sides to create grooves.

3. Roll the pink, blue, white and yellow icing as thinly as possible under your fingers. Cut into irregular lengths to shape giant sprinkles. Place on a sheet of baking paper or board and leave both the cake and sprinkles to harden overnight.

4. Turn the cake the right way up and place on a plate. Pack the cake crumbs mixture onto the top of the cake, doming it up in the centre as though reforming the natural cake shape.

5. Beat the fondant icing sugar with about 5 teaspoons of cold water to make a slightly runny paste. Spoon over the top of the cake and scatter with the giant sprinkles. Roll the red icing into a ball and position on top of the cake. Brush with confectioners' glaze.

TOP TIP

Confectioners' glaze, available from cake decorating websites, is used to give a glossy sheen, or brush the icing lightly with runny honey instead.

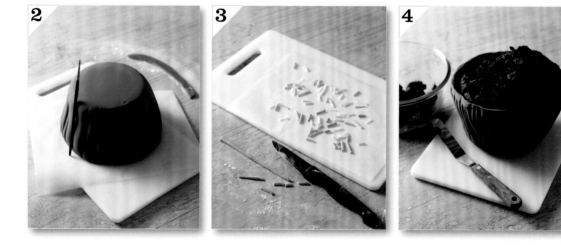

Grasshopper Cake

SERVES 8

◆ Preparation time:
25 minutes, plus cooling

◆ Cooking time:
1¼ hours

◆ Decoration time:
20 minutes

INGREDIENTS

✹ 250 ml/9 fl oz milk

✹ 1 tbsp lemon juice

✹ 280 g/10 oz self-raising flour

✹ 2 tbsp cocoa powder

✹ 1 tsp bicarbonate of soda

✹ 100 g/3½ oz butter, softened, plus extra for greasing

✹ 225 g/8 oz caster sugar

✹ 2 large eggs

✹ 100 g/3½ oz plain chocolate, melted

✹ 25 g/1 oz milk chocolate, grated, to decorate

FROSTING

✹ 200 g/7 oz unsalted butter, softened

✹ 250 ml/9 fl oz double cream

✹ 400 g/14 oz icing sugar, sifted

✹ 1 tsp peppermint extract

✹ few drops of green food colouring

Named after a Crème de Menthe cocktail, this decadent gateau is made up of layers of rich moist chocolate cake with a creamy mint-flavoured buttercream frosting.

1. Preheat the oven to 160°C/325°F/Gas Mark 3. Grease and line a 20-cm/8-inch round deep cake cake tin (see page 7).

2. Pour the milk into a jug and add the lemon juice. Leave for 15 minutes – the milk will start to curdle but this is ok.

3. Sift the flour, cocoa powder and bicarbonate of soda into a large bowl. Add the butter, caster sugar and eggs and pour in the milk mixture. Beat with an electric handheld whisk until thoroughly combined. Whisk in the melted chocolate.

4. Spoon the mixture into the prepared tin and smooth the surface. Bake in the preheated oven for about 1¼ hours, or until the cake is risen and a skewer inserted into the centre comes out clean. Cool in the tin for 20 minutes then turn out onto a wire rack to cool completely.

5. For the frosting, place the butter in a bowl and beat with an electric handheld whisk for 2–3 minutes until pale and creamy. Beat in two thirds of the cream then gradually beat in the icing sugar. Add the rest of the cream and continue beating for 1–2 minutes until the buttercream is very light and fluffy. Stir in the peppermint extract and enough food colouring to give a pale green colour.

6. Slice the cake horizontally into three equal rounds. Sandwich the rounds together with half the buttercream frosting. Spread the remaining buttercream over the top and sides of the cake. Decorate with the chocolate shavings.

TOP TIP

For an alcoholic version, flavour the buttercream with a couple of spoonfuls of Crème de Menthe instead of the peppermint extract.

CELEBRATION
CAKES

3

Chocolate Birthday Cake

SERVES 34

◆ Preparation time:
1 hour, plus cooling
◆ Cooking time:
4½ hours
◆ Decoration time:
2 hours, plus overnight setting

INGREDIENTS

✳ 100 g/3½ oz each of plain, milk and white chocolate, chopped and kept separate
✳ 20-cm/8-inch, 15-cm/6-inch and 10-cm/4-inch round rich chocolate cakes, see page 10
✳ 1 quantity white chocolate ganache, see page 16
✳ 3 quantities dark chocolate ganache, see page 16

With minor adjustments, this fabulous chocolate-packed coming of age cake can be adapted to suit any birthday by simply using the appropriate numbers to replace the 2s and 1s.

1. Line a baking sheet or chopping board with baking paper. Melt the plain chocolate (see page 16). Trace ten each of the '2' and '1' templates (see pages 94–95) on a piece of paper. Slide the tracing under the baking paper.

2. Put the melted plain chocolate in a small piping bag (see page 9) and snip off just the tip so the chocolate flows in a fine line. Pipe over the outlines of the numbers and then fill in the centres to make solid shapes. Repeat this process with both the milk and white chocolate. Leave in a cool place for several hours or overnight to set.

3. Slice each chocolate cake in half horizontally and sandwich each with the white chocolate ganache. Place the largest cake on a flat plate and the smaller ones on 15-cm/6-inch and 10-cm/4-inch cake cards.

4. Spread a thin layer of dark chocolate ganache around the sides of all three cakes with a palette knife to seal in the crumbs. Chill in the refrigerator for 15 minutes. Stack the medium cake, still on its cake card, on top of the largest cake and then stack the smallest cake, still on its cake card, on top, dowelling the two lower tiers for support (see page 19). Using a palette knife, spread the remaining ganache all over the cakes in an even layer.

5. Carefully peel the paper away from the chocolate numbers and scatter the numbers over the cakes like confetti. Prop some numbers up, particularly on the top, to give height.

TOP TIP

The chocolate numbers can be piped up to a week in advance. Once set, place in layers in an airtight container, still on the paper, and store in a cool place until ready to use.

Music Lover's Birthday Cake

SERVES 26

◆ Preparation time:
30 minutes, plus cooling

◆ Cooking time:
45–50 minutes

◆ Decoration time:
1¼ hours, plus over
48 hours setting

INGREDIENTS

✸ 100 g/3½ oz black
ready-to-roll icing,
see page 15

✸ icing sugar, for dusting

✸ 2 x 25-cm/10-inch
round vanilla sandwich
cakes, see page 11

✸ 7 tbsp raspberry or
strawberry jam

✸ 2 quantities
buttercream, see page 14

✸ 900 g/2 lb white ready-
to-roll icing, see page 15

✸ ½ quantity royal icing,
see page 15

✸ 1.3 m/4¼ feet black
ribbon, 3 mm/⅛ inch wide

✸ black food colouring

Eye-catching and effective, this simple cake will appeal to anyone with a love of music! You will need to allow at least two days for the notes on the top of the cake to harden.

1. Line a baking sheet with baking paper. Roll out the black icing thinly on a surface very lightly dusted with icing sugar. Cut out three 6-cm x 5-mm/2½- x ¼-inch sticks and three 2.5-cm/1-inch circles with a small round cutter. Using a rolling pin, gently roll the circles to stretch into oval shapes. Using the cutter, cut curved tips off the ends of the sticks. Moisten the cut areas with a dampened paintbrush and secure to the ovals to create simple note shapes. Transfer to the prepared sheet. Cut out three smaller circles using a 1-cm/½-inch cutter. Place on the sheet and leave all for at least 48 hours to harden.

2. Sandwich the cakes together with the jam and 8 tablespoons of the buttercream and place on a flat plate, preferably black or white. Using a palette knife, spread the top and sides of the cake with the remaining buttercream. Use the white icing to cover the cake (see page 18). Leave to firm up overnight before decorating, if desired.

3. Put the royal icing in a small piping bag and snip off just the tip (see page 9). Cut the ribbon

into 5 x 26-cm/10½-inch lengths and wrap one length around the middle of the cake, securing the ends with dots of icing from the piping bag. Secure two more ribbons either side of the first, leaving a slight gap between each.

4. Dilute a little black food colouring with a dash of water. Using a fine paintbrush, paint musical notes around the sides of the cake (see Top Tip).

5. Carefully peel the paper from the musical notes. Dot the base of the notes with a little icing from the piping bag and secure to the top of the cake. If necessary, support the notes by pushing a cocktail stick down into the cake behind the sticks until they set in position. Arrange the smaller circles between the notes.

TOP TIP
All you need to successfully paint the notes is a fine paintbrush and a fairly steady hand. For inspiration, get some sheet music to copy.

Dog Lover's Birthday Cake

SERVES 16

✦ Preparation time:
25 minutes, plus cooling

✦ Cooking time:
35–40 minutes

✦ Decoration time:
45 minutes, plus chilling

INGREDIENTS

✹ 2 x 20-cm/8-inch round vanilla sandwich cakes, see page 11

✹ 5 tbsp raspberry or strawberry jam

✹ 2 quantities buttercream, see page 14

✹ 100 g/3½ oz white chocolate, chopped

✹ large bowl of multi-coloured sugar sprinkles

✹ 25 g/1 oz bright blue ready-to-roll icing, see page 15

✹ icing sugar, for dusting

✹ 50 cm/20 inch bright blue wired ribbon, about 4 cm/1½ inches wide

No animal lover could resist this gorgeous birthday cake, suitable for any party or small gathering. To display the cake at its best, choose a brightly coloured plate or stand and a matching ribbon.

1. Sandwich the cakes together with the jam and 6 tablespoons of the buttercream and place on a flat plate or cake stand. Using a palette knife, spread a thin layer of buttercream over the cake to seal in the crumbs. Chill in the refrigerator for 15 minutes then spread the remaining buttercream over the cake.

2. Trace the Scottie dog template (see pages 94–95) onto a sheet of paper. Place the tracing under a larger sheet of baking paper on a baking sheet or chopping board. Melt the chocolate (see page 16). Put in a small piping bag and snip off just the tip (see page 9). Pipe over the outline of the dog then slide the template under the paper and pipe more outlines. You will need about nine shapes for the cake (see Top Tip). Fill in the centres of the shapes with more chocolate.

3. While the chocolate is still soft, scatter generously with sugar sprinkles and leave in a cool place or chill in the refrigerator for 30 minutes.

4. Shake off the loose sprinkles from the chocolate. Roll out the blue icing thinly on a surface lightly dusted with icing sugar and cut out thin strips about 3 cm/1¼ inches long. Moisten the strips with a dampened paintbrush and press gently around the dogs' necks. Carefully peel the paper away from the chocolate and gently press the shapes against the sides of the cake. Scatter more sprinkles on the top of the cake and decorate with a large bow, made using the wired ribbon.

TOP TIP
If you make extra Scottie dogs, they make perfect treats for children at a big family party.

Gingerbread Party Cake

SERVES 14–16

◆ Preparation time:
30 minutes, plus cooling
◆ Cooking time:
1¾ hours
◆ Decoration time:
1 hour, plus chilling

INGREDIENTS

✳ 450 g/1 lb plain flour
✳ 2 tsp baking powder
✳ 2 tsp ground ginger
✳ 400 g/14 oz sultanas
✳ 225 g/8 oz lightly salted
butter, plus extra for
greasing
✳ finely grated rind of
1 orange
✳ 225 g/8 oz golden syrup
✳ 150 g/5½ oz light
muscovado sugar
✳ 4 eggs, beaten

GINGERBREAD FIGURES

✳ 85 g/3 oz lightly salted
butter, softened
✳ 85 g/3 oz light
muscovado sugar
✳ 2 egg yolks
✳ 4 tbsp golden syrup
✳ 200 g/7 oz plain flour,
plus extra for dusting
✳ 1 tsp ground ginger

TO DECORATE

✳ 2 quantities
buttercream, see page 14
✳ 55 g/2 oz plain
chocolate, chopped
✳ 85 g/3 oz each of red,
orange and green
ready-to-roll icing,
see page 15
✳ icing sugar, for dusting

**Kids of all ages will adore this fun cake,
brilliant for a birthday or party cake.**

1. Preheat the oven to 160°C/325°F/Gas Mark 3. Grease and line a 20-cm/8-inch round cake tin (see page 7). Sift the flour, baking powder and ginger into a bowl and stir in the sultanas. Heat the butter in a saucepan with the orange rind, syrup and muscovado sugar until the butter has just melted. Add to the dry ingredients with the eggs and beat with a wooden spoon until combined. Spoon into the prepared tin, smooth the surface and bake in the preheated oven for 1¼ hours, or until firm to the touch. Leave to cool in the tin and leave the oven on.

2. For the gingerbread figures, put all of the ingredients in a food processor and blend to a soft dough. Wrap in clingfilm and chill for 1 hour.

3. Place the cake on a serving plate. Using a palette knife, spread a thin layer of buttercream over the cake. Chill for 15 minutes then spread the remaining buttercream over the cake in an even layer.

4. Increase the oven temperature to 180°C/350°F/Gas Mark 4. Line a baking sheet with baking paper. Roll out the gingerbread

dough thinly on a floured surface and cut out gingerbread figures using a 12-cm/4½-inch cutter. Re-roll the trimmings and make six figures in total. Place three figures in a row on the prepared baking sheet and bake for 5–6 minutes until the dough is cooked but not beginning to colour. Lift up the paper at the leg ends of the figures and place a cardboard tube (the centre of a clingfilm roll is ideal) under the legs. Return to the oven for a further 5–7 minutes until golden. Leave to cool then cook the remaining three figures in the same way.

5. Place the figures around the edge of the cake, pressing them into the buttercream. Melt the chocolate (see page 16). Put in a small piping bag and snip off just the tip (see page 9).

6. To make streamers, thinly roll out half of the red, orange and green icings on a surface lightly dusted with icing sugar and cut into 5-mm/¼-inch wide strips. Roll the strips around a thin skewer to create curls. Slide the streamers off the skewer and drape around the gingerbread. Cut out party hat shapes from the remaining icings with a sharp knife or scalpel and position, securing with melted chocolate. Pipe features and buttons with more chocolate.

Balloon Cake

◆ Preparation time:
25 minutes, plus cooling
◆ Cooking time:
40 minutes
◆ Decoration time:
1 hour, plus chilling

INGREDIENTS
✹ 2 x carrot sandwich
cakes, see page 12
✹ 2 quantities cream
cheese frosting,
see page 14
✹ 375 g/13 oz lilac
ready-to-roll icing,
see page 15
✹ 225 g/8 oz each of pink
and green ready-to-roll
icing, see page 15
✹ icing sugar, for dusting
✹ birthday candles
(as many as needed
for the birthday year)
✹ 1 m/3⅓ feet green
or pink ribbon, 1 cm/
½ inch wide

Easy to make and colourful, this delicious cake is ideal for any child's birthday party.

1. Sandwich the two carrot cakes together with a quarter of the cream cheese frosting. Place the cake on a 28-cm/11-inch round cake board. Using a palette knife, spread a very thin layer of frosting over the top and sides of the cake to seal in the crumbs. Chill in the refrigerator for 15 minutes. Spread a thicker layer of the remaining frosting over the cake, smoothing flat with the knife.

2. Use 150 g/5½ oz of the lilac icing to cover the cake board (see page 19). Knead the trimmings with the remaining lilac icing. Roll out 100 g/3½ oz of each of the lilac, pink and green icings very thinly on a surface lightly dusted with icing sugar. Cut into 2-cm/¾-inch wide strips, each about 14 cm/5½ inches long. Lay one strip vertically down the side of the cake so the base of the strip meets the iced board and the other end rests over the top of the cake. Repeat with all the strips around the sides of the cake, alternating the colours and leaving a slight gap between each strip.

3. Take 30 g/1 oz pieces of the remaining icings and roll each piece into a ball shape, until you have four balls from each icing. Pinch each ball slightly on one side to mould into a balloon shape. For the knots, form tiny cone shapes of icing and mark a cross into the thick ends with a knife. Secure the cone-shaped ends to the balloons with a dampened paintbrush.

4. Arrange the candles on top of the cake and tuck the balloons around them. Wrap the ribbon around the cake board and secure with a dressmaker's pin.

TOP TIP
Cut shorter lengths of fine ribbon and loop around the 'knots' of some of the balloons and stream across the cake.

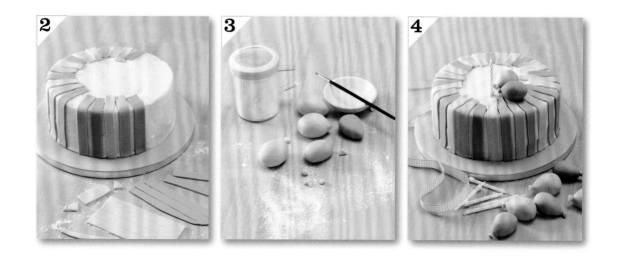

Lollipop Cake

SERVES 16

◆ Preparation time:
25 minutes, plus cooling
◆ Cooking time:
35–40 minutes
◆ Decoration time:
1 hour, plus overnight
setting

INGREDIENTS

✳ 2 x 18-cm/7-inch
square orange or
lemon sandwich cakes,
see page 11
✳ 1 quantity orange or
lemon buttercream,
see page 14
✳ 6 tbsp orange or
lemon curd
✳ 700 g/1 lb 9 oz yellow
ready-to-roll icing,
see page 15
✳ 150 g/5½ oz orange
ready-to-roll icing, see
page 15
✳ 24 yellow, orange, clear
and pink boiled sweets,
plus 12 lollipop sticks
✳ 1.5 m/5 feet each of
yellow, red and green
ribbon, each 1 cm/½ inch
wide, and 1.5 m/5 feet
of orange ribbon, 5 mm/
¼ inch wide

Colourful, fun and so easy to make, this cake is great for both boys and girls of all ages.

1. Sandwich the cakes with half of the buttercream and the fruit curd. Place on a 23-cm/9-inch square cake board. Using a palette knife, spread the remaining buttercream over the top and sides of the cake.

2. Use the yellow icing to cover the cake (see page 18). Use the orange icing to cover the cake board (see page 19). Leave to firm up overnight before decorating, if desired.

3. Preheat the oven to 200°C/400°F/Gas Mark 6. Line two baking sheets with baking paper. Place the boiled sweets in six stacks, spaced well apart, on one of the prepared sheets – each stack should contain two sweets of the same colour. Rest a lolly stick against each of the stacks.

4. Bake in the preheated oven for about 5 minutes, or until the sweets have melted just enough to spread around the sticks. Remove from the oven and push any areas of the sweets that have lost their round shape back in place with the edge of an oiled knife. Repeat with the other prepared sheet until you have 12 lollipops.

5. Leave for a few minutes before peeling the paper away and pressing the sticks into the cake. Wrap the yellow ribbon length around the cake board, securing with a dressmaker's pin, and the other ribbons around the cake, letting the ends trail or tying in bows.

TOP TIP
Watch closely when melting the sweets in the oven as they will suddenly turn very syrupy and lose their brightness.

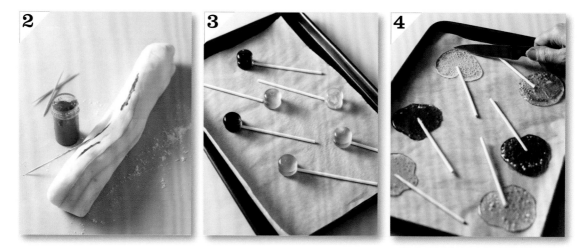

White Rose Wedding Cake

SERVES 28

◆ Preparation time:
1 hour, plus cooling
◆ Cooking time:
1 hour, 20 minutes
◆ Decoration time:
4 hours, plus 24 hours
setting

INGREDIENTS

✳ 1 kg/2 lb 4 oz white
ready-to-roll icing,
see page 15
✳ icing sugar, for dusting
✳ 150 g/5½ oz apricot
jam, plus 9 tbsp to glaze
✳ 2 quantites
buttercream, see page 14
✳ 2 x 20-cm/8-inch,
2 x 15-cm/6-inch and
2 x 10-cm/4-inch almond
or vanilla sandwich cakes,
see page 11
✳ 2 kg/4 lb 8 oz marzipan
✳ 4 quantities royal icing,
see page 15

Making this cake will help you to master the technique of modelling a simple sugar rose. Sugar roses are a little time consuming so a few evenings shaping them while watching TV is definitely the way to do it!

1. To make the roses, take a grape-sized piece of white ready-to-roll icing and shape into a cone, pressing the thick end down onto a board or work surface. Pinch in the cone around the base to form a 'waist'. Take a pea-sized ball of white icing and press it into a petal shape, pinching the icing between your thumb and forefinger until paper thin (dust your fingers lightly with icing sugar if the icing becomes sticky). Curl the petal around the cone to form the rose centre. Shape another slightly larger petal and wrap around the first. Continue layering the petals around the centre, increasing their size slightly and opening them out as you build up the rose. You'll need 6–8 petals in all. Slice the rose off the cone, about 1 cm/½ inch from the base, and place on a baking sheet lined with baking paper. Make the rest of the roses in the same way, varying the sizes of the cones and petals to make small and large roses until you have 22–25 roses altogether. Leave to harden, uncovered, for at least 24 hours.

2. Use the 150 g/5½ oz of jam, along with all the buttercream, to sandwich each pair of cakes together. Make apricot glaze with the remaining jam (see page 18). Place the smallest cake on a 10-cm/4-inch cake card, the medium cake on a 15-cm/6-inch card and the largest cake on a white cake stand. Brush the glaze over the cakes. Cover all the cakes with marzipan (see page 18), allowing 950 g/2 lb 2 oz for the largest cake, 650 g/1 lb 7 oz for the medium and 400 g/14 oz for the smallest. Leave overnight, uncovered, to firm up.

3. Dowel the two lower tiers and stack the cakes, still on their cake boards, using a little royal icing to hold the cakes in place (see page 19). Using a palette knife, spread the remaining royal icing in an even layer, texturing the surface slightly with the edge of the knife.

4. While the icing is still soft, gently press the roses into position so they form a trail that flows down one side of the cake.

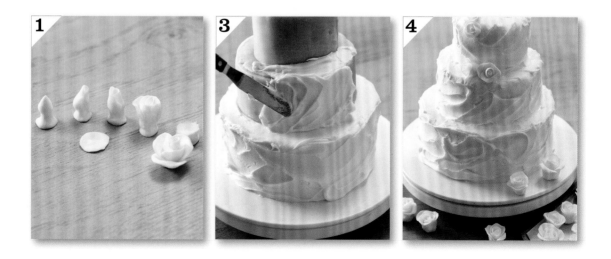

Black & White Wedding Cake

SERVES 50

◆ Preparation time:
55 minutes, plus cooling
◆ Cooking time:
4¾ hours
◆ Decoration time:
3½ hours, plus 24 hours
setting

INGREDIENTS

✳ 550 g/1 lb 4 oz
shop-bought chocolate
ready-to-roll icing
✳ icing sugar, for dusting
✳ 550 g/1 lb 4 oz white
chocolate, chopped
✳ 23-cm/9-inch and
18-cm/7-inch square
rich chocolate cakes,
see page 10
✳ 3 quantities white
chocolate ganache,
see page 16

This chocolate lover's dream wedding cake shows just how versatile and sculptural chocolate can be. Assemble the day before the wedding and store in a cool place.

1. To make the roses, break off small pieces of the chocolate icing and knead lightly until soft enough to mould. Use the icing to make large chocolate roses following the method on page 76. You will need 25 roses in total. Store in a cool place, covered loosely with clingfilm, for up to a week.

2. For the large cake collar, melt 350 g/12 oz of the chocolate (see page 16). Cut a rectangle out of card, 24 cm/9½ inches long and 1 cm/½ inch deeper than the cake. Line a chopping board with baking paper and pour the chocolate onto it. Using a palette knife, spread the chocolate out to a rectangle which measures at least 38 x 26 cm/15 x 10½ inches. Create texture with the edge of the palette knife and leave to set.

3. For the small cake collar, cut another piece of card, 19 cm/7½ inches long and 1 cm/½ inch deeper than the cake. Melt the remaining chocolate and line a second chopping board with baking paper. Spread the chocolate as above, this time to a rectangle which measures at least 38 x 21 cm/15 x 8¼ inches. Leave to set.

4. Place the large cake on a flat square plate and spread with about two thirds of the ganache. Place the small cake on an 18-cm/7-inch cake card and spread with the remaining ganache. Place the small cake on top of the large cake, in the centre.

5. Rest the large piece of card along one narrow edge of the large set chocolate rectangle and cut around it with a scalpel or sharp knife. Cut three more rectangles in the same way. Carefully peel the paper away from the chocolate, one rectangle at a time, and rest each against the sides of the cake so the corners meet. Cut out and secure the rectangles for the small cake in the same way.

6. Arrange the chocolate roses so there are nine on the top of the small cake and 16 around the edges of the large cake.

Bow Wedding Cake

SERVES 90

◆ Preparation time:
1 hour, 35 minutes,
plus cooling
◆ Cooking time:
10¼ hours
◆ Decoration time:
3 hours, plus 24 hours
setting

INGREDIENTS
✳ 225 g/8 oz apricot jam
✳ 25-cm/10-inch,
20-cm/8-inch and
15-cm/6-inch round rich
fruit cakes, see page 13
✳ 2.7 kg/6 lb marzipan
✳ 2.25 kg/5 lb white
ready-to-roll icing,
see page 15
✳ 2 quantities royal icing,
see page 15
✳ 3.5 m/11½ feet white
ribbon, about 1 cm/
½ inch wide
✳ icing sugar, for dusting

This delicate, stylish cake design is less time consuming than most wedding cakes but looks really stunning. The bow decoration could be replaced by ribbon or fabric bows that match the chosen colour scheme, making the cake even easier!

1. Make apricot glaze with the jam (see page 18). Brush over the cakes and cover with marzipan (see page 18), allowing 1.2 kg/2 lb 10 oz for the largest cake, 900 g/2 lb for the medium cake and 650 g/1 lb 7 oz for the smallest cake. Place the largest cake on a 33-cm/13-inch cake board, the medium on a 20-cm/8-inch cake card and the smallest on a 15-cm/6-inch cake card. Leave to set overnight.

2. Reserve 100 g/3½ oz of the white icing. Cover the cakes with the remainder (see page 18), allowing 900 g/2 lb for the largest cake, 700 g/1 lb 9 oz for the medium cake and 550 g/1 lb 4 oz for the smallest. Use the icing trimmings to cover the large cake board (see page 19). Dowel the two lower tiers for support (see page 19) and then stack the cakes, still on their cake boards, in position, using a little royal icing to hold the cakes in place. Leave to firm up overnight before decorating, if desired.

3. Put a little of the royal icing in a small piping bag fitted with a writer nozzle (see page 9). Wrap ribbon around the base of each cake, trimming and securing with dots of icing from the piping bag. Use the remaining royal icing to pipe tiny dots all over the tops and sides of the cakes.

4. For the bow ends, roll out the remaining white icing thinly on a surface lightly dusted with icing sugar. Cut the icing into 4-cm/1½-inch wide strips. Cut 2 x 5-cm/2-inch lengths from the strips and pinch both together at one of the short ends. Lightly dampen the top edge of the bottom cake tier and press the pinched ends onto the cake.

5. For the loops, cut 2 x 9-cm/3½-inch lengths from the strips. Bring the short ends together and pinch. Secure over the bow ends, as above. Cut a 1-cm/½-inch square from the remaining icing and press gently onto the centre of the bow for the knotted area. Wrap the remaining ribbon around the cake board, securing with a dressmaker's pin.

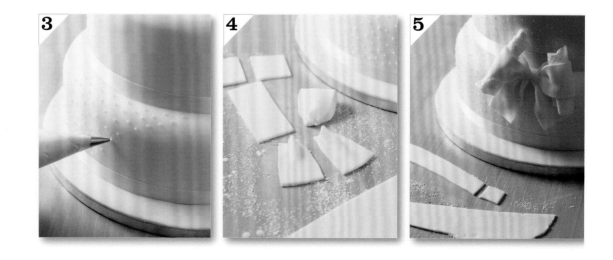

Red Velvet Valentine Cake

SERVES 16

◆ Preparation time:
40 minutes, plus cooling

◆ Cooking time:
25 minutes

◆ Decoration time:
1½ hours, plus setting

INGREDIENTS

✸ 280 g/10 oz self-raising flour

✸ 3 tbsp cocoa powder

✸ ½ tsp bicarbonate of soda

✸ 225 ml/8 fl oz buttermilk

✸ 2 tsp white wine vinegar

✸ 2 tsp vanilla extract

✸ 150 g/5½ oz lightly salted butter, softened, plus extra for greasing

✸ 200 g/7 oz light muscovado sugar

✸ 3 eggs

✸ 150 g/5½ oz raw beetroot, finely grated

✸ 2 quantities cream cheese frosting, see page 14

✸ 100 g/3½ oz plain chocolate, chopped

✸ 1 egg white

✸ 25–30 deep red edible flowers, such as pansies

✸ caster sugar, for dusting

The deeper the shades of red flowers you use for this cake, the more elegant it will be. Grated beetroot not only adds a delicious flavour and moist texture to the sponge, it complements the colours in the decoration.

1. Preheat the oven to 180°C/350°F/Gas Mark 4. Grease and line 3 x 20-cm/8-inch round sandwich cake tins (see page 7). Sift the flour, cocoa and bicarbonate of soda into a bowl. Mix together the buttermilk, vinegar and vanilla in a jug.

2. Put the butter and muscovado sugar in a large mixing bowl and beat with an electric mixer until pale and creamy. Beat in the eggs, one at a time (add a spoonful of the flour mixture if the contents start to separate). Stir in the beetroot.

3. Add the buttermilk mixture slowly to the flour mixture, stirring continuously until combined. Stir in the beetroot mixture until combined. Divide the mixture evenly among the prepared tins and bake in the preheated oven for 25 minutes, or until just firm to the touch. Transfer the cakes to a wire rack to cool.

4. Sandwich the cakes together with a third of the cream cheese frosting and spread the remainder over the top and sides with a palette knife. Use the plain chocolate to make a chocolate collar (see page 17).

5. Beat 1 teaspoon of water with the egg white. To frost the flowers, gently pull a flower from its stem and use your fingers or a paintbrush to coat both sides of each petal with a fine film of egg white. Sprinkle with the caster sugar, twisting and turning the flower so it's evenly coated. Place on a baking sheet lined with crumpled baking paper and frost the remaining flowers. Leave for several hours to dry before arranging over the cake.

TOP TIP

If you can't get small, whole flowers, rose petals also look effective. Separate the petals and frost as above.

4 **5** **5**

Valentine Hearts Cake

SERVES 16

◆ Preparation time:
25 minutes, plus cooling
◆ Cooking time:
35–40 minutes
◆ Decoration time:
3½ hours, plus overnight
setting

INGREDIENTS
✳ 100 g/3½ oz deep pink
ready-to-roll icing,
see page 15
✳ 250 g/9 oz deep red
ready-to-roll icing,
see page 15
✳ icing sugar, for dusting
✳ 2 x 20-cm/8-inch
vanilla or almond
sandwich cakes,
see page 11
✳ 1 quantity buttercream,
see page 14
✳ 6 tbsp raspberry jam
✳ 700 g/1 lb 9 oz white
ready-to-roll icing,
see page 15
✳ ½ quantity royal icing,
see page 15
✳ 80 cm/2½ feet pink
ribbon, preferably striped,
2.5–3 cm/1–1¼ inches
wide
✳ 1 m/3⅓ feet pink
ribbon, 1 cm/½ inch wide

This pretty cake is easy to assemble as long as you add the hearts in stages. Rushing the decoration will result in the hearts collapsing like a pack of cards!

1. To make the hearts, line a large baking sheet with baking paper. Roll out the pink icing and 100 g/3½ oz of the red icing thinly on a surface lightly dusted with icing sugar. Cut out heart shapes from half of these pink and red icings, using a 3-cm/1¼-inch heart-shaped cutter and transfer to the prepared sheet. Cut out larger hearts from the remaining rolled-out icings, using a 4-cm/1½-inch heart-shaped cutter. From each large heart, cut out a smaller heart from the middle, using a 2-cm/¾-inch cutter. Transfer all hearts and centres to the prepared sheet. You will need about 40 heart shapes altogether. Leave for several hours or overnight, uncovered, to harden.

2. Sandwich the cakes with half of the buttercream and all of the raspberry jam. Place on a 28-cm/11-inch cake board. Using a palette knife, spread the remaining buttercream over the top and sides of the cake.

3. Cover the cake with the white icing (see page 18). Cover the cake board with the remaining red icing (see page 19). Leave to firm up overnight before decorating, if desired. Put the royal icing in a small piping bag and snip off just the tip (see page 9).

4. Take a couple of the larger hearts from the paper and prop them up on the top of the cake, securing them to the cake and where they lean against each other with dots of icing from the piping bag. Prop up another two hearts slightly away from the first two and then a further two. Leave for at least an hour to set.

5. Once set, add all of the hearts to the cake, securing them at different angles and adding height to the centre of the cake. Do this in a few stages so the hearts have a chance to set.

6. Wrap the wider ribbon around the base of the cake, securing with a dot of royal icing. Wrap the thinner ribbon around the cake board, securing with a dressmaker's pin.

Trick or Treat Bucket

SERVES 16

✦ Preparation time:
30 minutes, plus cooling
✦ Cooking time:
40–50 minutes
✦ Decoration time:
1 hour, plus overnight
setting

INGREDIENTS

✹ 4 x 15-cm/6-inch round
orange sandwich cakes,
see page 11
✹ 1 quantity orange
buttercream, see page 14
✹ 9 tbsp orange curd
✹ 450 g/1 lb orange
ready-to-roll icing, see
page 15
✹ icing sugar, for dusting
✹ 85 g/3 oz each of white
and black ready-to-roll
icing, see page 15
✹ black food colouring or
black food colouring pen
✹ 250 g/9 oz mixed
sweets and cookies

**Not a cake to go out trick or treating with,
but then it's already packed full of goodies!**

1. Sandwich all the cakes together, spreading
2 tablespoons of buttercream and 3 tablespoons
of orange curd between each layer. Place the
cake on a chopping board and spread the
remaining buttercream over the top and sides
with a palette knife.

2. Measure around the circumference and
depth of the cake with two pieces of string. Roll
out the orange icing on a surface lightly dusted
with icing sugar to a rectangle which is slightly
longer than the circumference and 2.5 cm/1 inch
wider than the depth of the cake. Trim the edges
of the icing so it is the exact length and width
of the strings. Roll up the icing, reserving the
trimmings, and position it against the side of the
cake. Carefully unroll the icing around the cake
until the ends meet.

3. Trace and cut out the ghost template (see
pages 94–95). Thinly roll out the white icing
on a chopping board and cut around the
template using a sharp knife or scalpel. Brush
the underside of the shape with a dampened
paintbrush and secure to the orange icing. Make
and secure 6–7 more ghosts in the same way.

4. Roll out the black icing under your fingers
to a long, thin log about 1 cm/½ inch thick and
23 cm/9 inches long. Slice off the ends to neaten
and dampen the ends with the paintbrush.
Secure the ends of the icing over the top of the
bucket, pressing down firmly.

5. Shape a pumpkin using the remaining orange
icing, marking grooves around the sides with the
back of a knife. Use black food colouring and a
fine paintbrush, or a black food colouring pen, to
paint ghost eyes and pumpkin features. Pile the
cookies and candies on top of the cake, letting
some spill out onto the serving plate.

TOP TIP
For a neat finish, use an icing
smoother to give a flat, smooth look to
the orange icing around the cake.

Haunted House

SERVES 20

◆ Preparation time:
25 minutes, plus cooling
◆ Cooking time:
2 hours
◆ Decoration time:
1½ hours, plus overnight
setting

INGREDIENTS

✹ 50 g/1¾ oz white
ready-to-roll icing,
see page 15
✹ icing sugar, for dusting
✹ 200 g/7 oz plain
chocolate, chopped
✹ 50 g/1¾ oz orange
ready-to-roll icing,
see page 15
✹ small bowl of chocolate
sprinkles
✹ 18-cm/7-inch square
rich chocolate cake,
see page 10
✹ 2 quantities dark
chocolate ganache,
see page 16
✹ black food colouring or
black food colouring pen

This is a fun cake to attempt if you're in a creative mood for Halloween! Decorate up to 24 hours before Halloween and store in a cool place.

1. For the moon, roll out the white icing to a thickness of about 1 cm/½ inch on a surface lightly dusted with icing sugar. Cut out a circle using a 7.5-cm/3-inch cutter. Transfer to a piece of baking paper and leave overnight to set.

2. Melt 175 g/6 oz of the chocolate (see page 16). Trace and cut out the house, tree and window templates (see pages 94–95). Slide the house template under a piece of baking paper and the tree template under another larger piece. Put half the melted chocolate in a small piping bag and snip off the tip (see page 9). Pipe an outline around the house template and then around the tree. Slide the tree template under the paper and pipe six to eight more tree outlines, varying their heights (as indicated on template).

3. Place the remaining chocolate in the piping bag and thickly fill in the centres of the shapes, reserving some chocolate for decoration. While the chocolate is still soft, create four window

shapes from thinly rolled orange icing by cutting around the window template with a sharp knife or scalpel. Set aside the trimmings. Position the windows on the house. Scatter the tree branches with chocolate sprinkles. Pipe the remaining chocolate to create window panes and a front door on the house.

4. Place the cake on a chopping board. Swirl the ganache over the top and sides with a palette knife. While still soft, carefully peel the paper from the house and moon shapes and press them gently down into the cake.

5. Use the remaining orange icing to shape round pumpkin shapes, marking grooves around the sides with the back of a knife, and place around the cake. Use black food colouring and a fine paintbrush, or a black food colouring pen, to paint a bat onto the moon and faces onto the pumpkins. Surround the house with the trees.

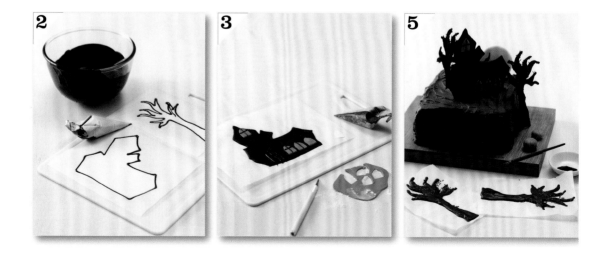

Christmas Stars & Berries

SERVES 30

◆ Preparation time:
30 minutes, plus cooling

◆ Cooking time:
3¼–3½ hours

◆ Decoration time:
1½ hours, plus 24 hours
setting

INGREDIENTS

✳ 900 g/2 lb white ready-
to-roll icing, see page 15

✳ icing sugar, for dusting

✳ 5 tbsp apricot jam

✳ 20-cm/8-inch round
rich fruit cake,
see page 13

✳ 900 g/2 lb marzipan

✳ 55 g/2 oz deep red
ready-to-roll icing,
see page 15

✳ 1 quantity royal icing,
see page 15

✳ red food colouring

✳ small bowl of silver
balls, in two or three sizes

✳ 80 cm/2½ feet red
ribbon, 2 cm/¾ inch wide

✳ 1 m/3⅓ feet white,
red or silver ribbon,
1 cm/½ inch wide

**Simple, fresh and modern, this is the perfect
cake design if you don't have a lot of time to ice
and decorate your Christmas cake.**

1. To make the stars, line a baking sheet or
board with baking paper. Roll out 55 g/2 oz of
the white icing thinly on a surface lightly dusted
with icing sugar. Cut out star shapes using
small star-shaped cutters measuring about
2–4 cm/¾–1½ inches across. Transfer to the
prepared sheet. There should be about 14 stars
in total. Leave for several hours or overnight,
uncovered, to harden.

2. Make apricot glaze with the jam (see page
18). Brush over the cake and cover with the
marzipan (see page 18). Leave to set overnight.
Place on a 28-cm/11-inch cake board. Reserve
150 g/5½ oz of the white icing and use the
remainder to cover the cake (see page 18). Use
the reserved white icing to cover the cake board
(see page 19). Leave to firm up overnight before
decorating, if desired.

3. Cut the red icing in half and roll under your
fingers into two thin logs, each about 1 cm/
½ inch wide. Slice the logs into 1 cm/½ inch thick
pieces and roll each piece into the shape of a
small berry. Scatter up to 15 berries over the top
of the cake.

4. Colour half of the royal icing with the red
colouring. Put the red and white royal icing
separately into two small piping bags fitted with
writer nozzles (see page 9). Use the red icing to
pipe lines around the edges of the stars. Arrange
the stars on top of the cake, propping some up
against the berries and securing in place with
dots of white royal icing.

5. Scatter silver balls over the cake and board,
securing those that roll around with dots of
white royal icing. Wrap the red ribbon around
the base of the cake, securing with dots of royal
icing. Wrap the other ribbon around the cake
board, securing with a dressmaker's pin.

TOP TIP
A two quantity batch of royal icing can
be spread over the cake, instead of the
ready-to-roll icing, if you prefer.

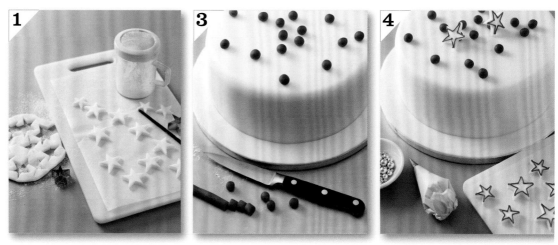

Winter Wonderland

SERVES 30

♦ Preparation time:
30 minutes, plus cooling
♦ Cooking time:
3¼–3½ hours
♦ Decoration time:
1½ hours, plus 24 hours
setting

INGREDIENTS
✳ 250 g/9 oz white ready-
to-roll icing, see page 15
✳ icing sugar, for dusting
✳ 4 tbsp apricot jam
✳ 20-cm/8-inch round
rich fruit cake,
see page 13
✳ 900 g/2 lb marzipan
✳ 700 g/1 lb 9 oz pale
blue ready-to-roll icing,
see page 15
✳ 150 g/5½ oz dark blue
ready-to-roll icing, see
page 15
✳ 1 quantity royal icing,
see page 15
✳ 1 m/3⅓ feet blue or
white ribbon, 1 cm/
½ inch wide

This simple cake makes such a pretty centrepiece for the Christmas dinner table. It also works equally well using a vanilla sponge cake, sandwiched with buttercream and apricot jam before icing.

1. To make the trees, line a baking sheet or board with baking paper. Roll out the white icing thinly on a surface lightly dusted with icing sugar and cut out tree shapes using small cutters (see Top Tip). Transfer to the prepared sheet. You will need roughly 12 trees altogether. Leave overnight, uncovered, to harden.

2. Make apricot glaze with the jam (see page 18). Brush over the cake and cover with marzipan (see page 18). Leave to set overnight. Place on a 28-cm/11-inch cake board. Use the pale blue icing to cover the cake (see page 18). Use the dark blue icing to cover the cake board (see page 19). Leave to firm up overnight before decorating, if desired.

3. Put the royal icing in a piping bag fitted with a writer nozzle (see page 9). Use to pipe tiny dots over the trees to resemble snowflakes.

4. Pipe a little royal icing along the bases of the trees and secure to the top of the cake, supporting them briefly until you feel they can stand upright. If the trees start to lean over, they can be supported by pushing a cocktail stick gently into the icing behind them and leaving until the trees have set before removing.

5. Use more royal icing from the bag to pipe dots over the top of the cake, thinning the dots out towards the top edge of the cake. Pipe further dots around the base of the cake and board. Wrap the ribbon around the cake board, securing with a dressmaker's pin.

TOP TIP
This cake looks effective if using two or three different tree-shaped cutters in slightly different shapes and sizes.

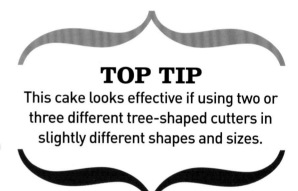

Templates

Fill with
chocolate
to this line
for shorter
trees